Social work, domestic violence and child protection

Challen...

Catherine H...

The POLICY PRESS

First published in Great Britain in 2000 by

The Policy Press
University of Bristol
34 Tyndall's Park Road
Bristol BS8 1PY
UK

Tel   +44 (0)117 954 6800
Fax   +44 (0)117 973 7308
E-mail tpp@bristol.ac.uk
http://www.bristol.ac.uk/Publications/TPP

ISBN 1 86134 190 3

Catherine Humphreys is a Lecturer in the Department of Social Policy and Social Work, University of Warwick.

Cover design by Qube Design Associates, Bristol
Printed in Great Britain by Hobbs the Printers Ltd, Southampton

Contents

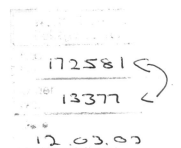

Acknowledgements

I would like to thank the social workers from Coventry Social Services who cooperated with this research. It is not easy to have work scrutinised by an outside observer who is involved in neither the day-to-day tensions of child protection work, nor the difficulties of being restructured with the subsequent loss of team members. The patience and openness of all members of the teams involved was greatly appreciated.

I would like also to thank Birgitta Lundberg and other members of the Child Protection Unit who supported and sponsored the work.

Jivan Sembi, Anne Hossack, Deborah Carter and Satish Thakor as manager and team leaders paved the way and encouraged the research process with their teams.

Norma Baldwin assisted and encouraged the original initiative, and Kate Brown and Becky Jones followed through with the process of dissemination. Their facilitation of the research was much appreciated.

I would also acknowledge that both policy and practice has moved on in the local authority since this work was undertaken. However, the continued interest in this research by many social services departments and interagency forums has led to the publication of this research report with attendant updates of work which is now occurring in the areas specified in the different chapters. Such wide-ranging interest is testimony to the relevance of local authorities sponsoring and allowing access for research purposes. It is appreciated that the department did not place barriers to this research and its dissemination.

The views expressed here are those of the author and do not necessarily represent the views of the organisations involved in the research.

Executive summary

The research project was developed in conjunction with the Child Protection Unit, Coventry Social Services, and arose out of concerns which were surfacing about child protection interventions where domestic violence was a feature of the child's family. The connections between child abuse and domestic violence had been identified, but details of how these concerns might be translated into practice have been slower to follow. This project was established to overview current practice, and to highlight the issues that need attention if work in this area was to be progressed.

Research design

Documentary analysis of case files and semi-structured interviews with workers were undertaken to gain an understanding of child protection intervention where domestic violence featured in the child's life. Thirty-two files involving 93 children who were the subject of a child protection conference were examined. Every file was examined for those Asian families from two children's and families' teams who participated in a child protection conference during a two-year period (January 1994-December 1995). Of these cases 12 involved domestic violence. The point needs to be clearly made that the disproportionate number of Asian families is due to a sampling technique that sought to highlight the particular issues faced by Asian families working with child protection professionals. The 20 non-Asian files were selected over a three-year period (January 1994-December 1996) from the same two teams. Social workers who had worked with each of the families were interviewed.

Emerging patterns

Two overall themes emerged in the research: intervention either avoided or minimised the issues of domestic violence in the family (the dominant pattern), or took a confrontational approach which involved the most serious intervention strategies of removing the children.

Physical injury to the child's mother

Within this sample, 'the atrocity story' of severe physical abuse appeared to dominate responses to domestic violence while less visible forms of violence and control tended to be ignored. Eleven out of the 32 women in this study were reported to have severe injuries as a result of incidents of domestic violence. While the attention to health problems that women face from serious assaults needs to be highlighted, both for the woman's sake as well as from the perspective of her children, there are also problems that arise if domestic violence becomes identified only with serious physical assault.

Strategies for minimising violence

The research pointed to a range of strategies through which social workers and other professionals avoided domestic violence.

In the *assessment process* this included: supporting the man as the cornerstone of the family, rather than challenging his abuse; inappropriately naming the mother's violence as more of a, or as great a, problem as the man's violence towards her; diverting to other issues such as mental health or alcohol abuse; and ignoring the man in the assessment process. There were also a series of *reporting strategies* which made domestic violence invisible. These included: reports failing to mention domestic violence as a relevant issue, although the case notes show that it is occurring; minimising language, such as 'marital conflict' or 'an argument between the parents' to describe a violent assault.

The tendency to minimise violence can render practice ineffectual as core issues which affect the family's functioning are ignored.

More recently, a number of strategies have been developed to counteract the tendency for domestic violence to become invisible. Several local authorities have developed mechanisms for *screening and monitoring* for domestic violence; *specialist training* has been developed; and *procedures and protocols* for both interagency working and work within specific organisations has also been helpful in providing clearer guidelines for workers.

Adult mental health

In this sample of 32 cases there were three men cited with mental health problems and 13 women. However, these problems were given little attention unless they were seen to directly affect child protection issues. Little connection was made between mental health issues for women and domestic violence.

Of the 12 Asian families in which domestic violence was an issue, five women and three men were reported with mental health problems.

The numbers of women in this study suffering from impaired mental health, particularly where domestic violence was an issue, suggest that child protection workers need to give this issue much greater consideration. Particular attention is needed to gain appropriate mental health assessments and intervention for Asian men and women.

Alcohol abuse and domestic violence

The dilemmas in working with the link between domestic violence and alcohol or drug abuse pose particular problems for intervention in this area. In

18 of the cases alcohol abuse by the mother's partner is named as a problem. In seven cases the mother's alcohol or drug abuse is named as a problem. Frequently, the focus of the child protection inquiry became the mother's alcohol abuse, and the connection between this abuse and domestic violence was rarely made.

Challenging men

Shifting the focus of child protection onto the man and his violence provides a continuing challenge to each of the professionals involved where domestic violence is an issue. The tendency to focus on the mother and her problems is a familiar and yet inappropriate pattern in child protection intervention when domestic violence is an issue of child abuse.

Approximately half the sample had no child protection intervention which even potentially addressed the man's violence. The most useful were strategies that occurred within a legal framework, while the evidence from this sample showed that most other attempts were ineffective.

The attendance of domestic violence offenders at child protection conferences

In 11 cases in this sample, where male violence towards the mother was/or had been an issue, the father attended the case conference either alone or with the mother present.

In nine of these cases, domestic violence was not mentioned in the case plan, and if it was discussed at conference the issue was avoided or minimised.

The issue of conference attendance is complex. Future practice needs to address the issue of safety and pre-conference planning with the woman to take account of the issues of domestic violence.

Children's issues

Paradoxically, most social workers argued that their focus was the child and their ability to recognise and intervene in the 'adult's issues' were secondary to this focus. However, the attention to the child was often minimal, with little work undertaken to represent their views directly or indirectly at conferences; little individualised assessment of the resilience or negative impact of domestic violence on their lives; only two referrals for counselling follow-up; and problems with child contact arrangements. Future practice with children in situations of domestic violence will confront these issues creatively and give greater individualised attention to their needs.

Practical and emotional support for women

The level of emotional and practical support which is available to women when faced with difficult decisions about their future is constantly referred to as a crucial factor in determining the confidence with which women pursue their options. In this sample, there was considerable pressure placed on women to separate or remain separated from violent men if they wanted to retain residency with their children. However, the practical and emotional supports which might have made this possible were often inadequate. Directions for good practice lie in creating much stronger partnerships with women so that the safety issues for themselves and their children can be addressed.

Accommodation of children

In this sample, 16 (50%) families had children who were accommodated by the local authority or, in the case of an older child, privately accommodated. This involved 41 children, who spent periods of time in voluntary placement and short placements on Emergency Protection Orders (EPO), through to children being freed for adoption. In another eight cases mothers were warned at a strategy meeting or case conferences that if the man returned, "the children would be accommodated, an EPO made, or [there would be] an immediate return to conference at which decisions would be made about the future of the children."

Though questions could be raised about the focus of intervention prior to accommodation, and the degree to which social workers attempted to establish a partnership with the woman before using 'threats', the high levels of accommodation of children in this sample do not necessarily suggest

that children were being inappropriately accommodated. Rather, male violence created a particularly vulnerable group of women and children. In this sample it was frequently a factor associated with mothers losing their children either temporarily or permanently. Sometimes this was a direct relationship, more often an indirect association.

Worker safety

An issue which is frequently overlooked in discussions of child protection is worker protection. In this sample there were 11 reported instances of abusive incidents to workers. Particular risks appeared to be involved when children were being accommodated or decisions had been made not to rehabilitate the children to the family. Generally, there was a tendency to underestimate the risks posed by women and other family members to workers.

In the future, should there be a shift to more proactive work with men, there would need to be an attendant shift in the security offered to workers.

Conclusion

The research suggests that practice in this area is both changing and very varied, with examples of good practice as well as some worrying examples of poor practice.

In general, it is suggested that two principles guide the development of policy and intervention in the area of domestic violence and child abuse. Firstly, developing interventions which direct responsibility towards the man and his abuse. Secondly, progressing the idea that protecting and supporting the child's mother in situations of domestic violence is also good child protection. This research highlighted the fact that there were significant barriers to realising these principles in practice which will need to be addressed to progress future work in this area.

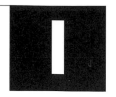

Setting the context: domestic violence and child abuse

The connections between the abuse of women and the abuse of children are now well recognised. However, the ways in which intervention and services which focus on child abuse can be structured to take into account both the needs of children and of their mothers is an issue which is emerging as a pivotal one in responding appropriately to this knowledge. This report explores the problems and the opportunities presented to statutory social workers responding to child abuse which occurred in the context of violence towards the child's mother. Research was undertaken with two children's and families' teams in Coventry Social Services Department and the findings from this research form the basis of the report. Since the research project has been completed (1997), further work has been undertaken throughout the UK and each chapter will draw on areas in which innovative practice has occurred.

What is domestic violence?

The term 'domestic violence' is a contested one. On the one hand, it names explicitly violence in the home and does not cover up this violence with terms such as 'relationship conflict'. It is also a term in common usage and therefore provides a convenient and well recognised shorthand. On the other hand, although the term has the advantage of covering a range of relationships in which violence occurs – including between gay and lesbian couples, women's violence against men, and violence by other family relatives, both men and women, in extended families (Hendessai, 1999) – the gendered nature of domestic violence is hidden by the term.

Between 80-97% of domestic violence is directed towards women (Mayhew et al, 1993, p 83). Even studies such as that undertaken by the Home Office (Mirrlees-Black, 1999), which on a self-completion questionnaire showed relatively similar levels of recent domestic assault in the last year by both men and women, makes the point that this did not mean that men were equally victimised:

Men were less upset by their experience, considerably less frightened, less often injured, and less likely to seek medical help. (Mirrlees-Black, 1999, p 61)

The term 'violence' is also often associated with physical attack, whereas the forms of abuse experienced by women from known men cover a range of abusive behaviours. These include among other things: sexual abuse, economic deprivation such as keeping the woman without food or money, intimidation, threats, emotional abuse through undermining and belittling comments, isolation, humiliation, using or abusing the children to force compliance from the woman, and a myriad of other ways in which dominance and control are enforced to position the woman in a role of subservience. Cultural, religious and social context may increase the impact and range of abusive strategies that can be directed at women (Mama, 1989; Bhatti-Sinclair, 1994), as can the issues of disability (Mullender, 1996). The term covers a wide range of relationships through which mostly women are abused. These include abuse by husbands, boyfriends, partners, ex-partners, fathers, sons and other close relatives, particularly of the husband. Domestic violence occurs across all communities irrespective of race, culture, religion, social class or age (Eekelaar and Katz, 1978; Dobash and Dobash, 1980).

While it has been essential to highlight the seriousness of domestic violence and its effects on women and children, it is also noticeable that as service provision increases and the issue is debated more publicly, we are seeing a wider range of complex issues emerging as a more diverse group of women step forward. The 'pure victim' is less discernable. Davies et al (1998) in their discussion of safety planning clearly make the point:

> ... not all of them [women] experienced extreme physical violence or psychological abuse. They were not necessarily terrified of their abuser. Instead, they had more varied sets of experience and needs for assistance, protection, and support, which they understood in complex ways. (Davies et al, 1998, p 17)

> The term domestic violence, as used in this report, can be understood as the misuse of power and the exercise of control by one individual over another – generally by men over women – with whom they have been in an intimate relationship. It assumes a wide range of abusive physical, sexual and psychological behaviours.

Currently, Britain has not undertaken a national prevalence study. However, the smaller, local studies reflect similar prevalence to national studies in other countries. Mooney's study in North London (1994) found that one in four women surveyed had experienced domestic violence sometime in their lives, while one in 10 had experienced an incident in the past 12 months. These figures are identical to those of the national Canadian prevalence study of 12,300 women. The British Crime Survey has shown remarkably consistent homicide rates over the past 10 years with two thirds of women being killed by partners or ex-partners (as against 9% of deaths of men), an average of almost two women a week.

Post-separation violence is also an issue which needs to be made explicit, particularly in the context of this report, where there was often evidence of significant pressure placed on women to separate from violent men, often with little consideration of the continued risks towards both them and their

children. A study by the Home Office (Kelly, 1999) showed that one third of domestic violence calls to the police come from women who are separated. Moreover, one third of the women who are murdered have already separated, with a US study by Wilson and Daly (1992) of homicide showing that the actual process of separation was the most dangerous time for women.

The relationship between domestic violence and child abuse

Child abuse is now clearly linked with domestic violence. The research shows a number of issues of grave concern (see Parkinson and Humphreys, 1998). Children themselves may be killed by men who are also violent towards their mothers (O'Hara, 1994). Child death enquiries show a significant number of cases in which the child's death occurred in the context of the man's violence towards the child's mother, or other significant carers (James, 1994). Many men who abuse women may also physically abuse children with an overlap in the range of between 45-70% depending on the study (Bowker et al, 1988; Stark and Flitcraft, 1988). There is also evidence to suggest increased prevalence of child sexual abuse in cases of domestic violence (Forman, 1995). Hence, the incidence of domestic violence is high for children on the child protection register, and this incidence may double when active monitoring and screening occurs (Farmer and Owen, 1995; Hester and Pearson, 1998). Women themselves are also more likely to punish their children more harshly, frequently either to prevent a worse beating from the abusive man, or because they themselves are at the 'end of their tether' with managing their own stress and fear (Mullender, 1996). Pregnancy is a vulnerable time when violence may commence or escalate (Mezey, 1997). A survey conducted in GP waiting rooms in Hackney showed that 2% of women surveyed reported a miscarriage as a result of violence (Stanko et al, 1998).

Children may also suffer indirectly, even when not directly abused themselves. Children are usually aware of the abuse towards their mothers (Hughes, 1998; Abrahams, 1994). While there is no recognisable syndrome, with each child reacting differently depending upon their age, support networks, gender, personal resilience and other protective factors in their lives, there are heightened levels of distress in this group of children. One study showed 2.5 times the rate of behavioural and psychological problems of other children in a control group (Wolfe et al, 1985). Children may recover once they feel safe and when their mothers are in a less debilitating situation where they are more able to meet the children's physical and emotional needs (Wolfe et al, 1986). However, there are also problems created for children through disruption to their family networks, schools, and friendship networks (Mullender et al, 1998). There may be additional issues for black and ethnic minority children who move away from a local community which offers protection against racism (Imam, 1994) or where there are increased risks of abduction and deportation (Patel, 1997). Disabled children are particularly vulnerable to disruption if their homes, schools or care packages have been tailored to accommodate their needs.

In short, the risks posed to women and children through male violence are such that where child abuse is present, then questions need to be raised about violence towards the child's mother; and similarly, child abuse should be actively considered as a possibility when domestic violence is present.

The statutory child welfare context

Professionals in statutory child welfare have often been criticised for their inadequate response to domestic violence. Social workers in particular have been taken to task for ignoring violence towards the child's mother unless the child was directly harmed (Maynard, 1985); for ignoring the effects on children of witnessing domestic violence (Brandon and Lewis, 1996); for focusing on the mother's 'failure to protect', or other problems, rather than the man's violence (Milner, 1993; Lloyd, 1995); for being slow to recognise the link between domestic violence and child abuse (Stark and Flitcraft, 1988); and for paying little attention to the specific issues which black women may have in accessing help (Mama, 1989).

Social work responses have not been helped by the Children Act (1989) which fails to make any mention of domestic violence. The checklist of children's wishes and feelings, for example, fails to make reference to issues of domestic violence (unlike legislation in other countries). Assessment guidance originally overlooked the issue as well.

A signal of a change in orientation occurred in 1994 when the Social Services Inspectorate (SSI) held two significant conferences which placed domestic violence on the agenda for future action within the statutory childcare sector (Ball, 1995). A number of initiatives followed in the 1990s, with numerous conference and training days held by Women's Aid, children's charities and interagency forums on the issues of child abuse and domestic violence. The Department of Health (DoH) continued to keep the issue on the childcare agenda issuing a consultation document on interagency cooperation (DoH, 1998). In this document it states:

> *We now have a growing awareness of the seriousness of domestic violence as a social problem and the damaging effect that it can have on the health and development of children who are exposed to it. (DoH, 1998, p 11)*

Other initiatives have included the commissioning by the DoH of a training pack and reader on children and domestic violence (Hester et al, 1999), and new assessment guidance which names the issue of domestic violence.

In general, it is suggested that two principles guide the development of policy and intervention in the area of domestic violence and child abuse.

> Firstly, developing interventions which direct responsibility towards the man and his abuse. Secondly, progressing the idea that protecting and supporting the child's mother in situations of domestic violence is also good child protection.

The refocusing debate

Given the prevalence of domestic violence and its destructive effects on women and children, issues are raised about the most effective form of intervention, particularly by the statutory childcare agency. Clearly, not all children living in situations of domestic violence should be the subject of a child protection enquiry under Section 47 of the 1989 Children Act. The British Crime Survey (Mayhew et al, 1993), in a conservative estimate, suggests that there are 530,000 assaults of women by men in the home each year and that in 90% of cases children are in the adjacent room. While recognising that these situations are potentially damaging to children (as well as women and sometimes men), the process of investigating and conferencing all incidents would divert immense resources into this area which could more effectively be directed to crisis intervention and long-term services for women and children. Women's Aid, the children's charities and the DoH (often for differing reasons) have all advocated re-balancing the focus for the work with children and their families towards supporting the broader welfare needs of the child (Section 17), rather than concentrating only on investigations of incidents of abuse. Potentially this would mean categorising children living with domestic violence as children in need, and providing supportive services accordingly.

In spite of the potentially powerful convergence of pressure from the DoH (1995), the large children's charities and Women's Aid Federations towards a greater emphasis on support rather than investigation, the shift in service orientation has proved to be far from straightforward. Firstly, there has been very little new money from the DoH or other government agencies to fund and service the shift in focus. An overview of children's services plans in 1998 for one region (N=21) showed that only eight made any mention at all of domestic violence, and only three gave any attention to resources, and services for women and children living with domestic violence. All plans named the problems which authorities face in attempting to refocus services towards family support.

A further powerful influence in shaping the children and families agenda have been child death enquiries (James, 1994). Child death enquiries have driven social work towards a greater focus on risk assessment, specifically as to whether children are at risk of significant harm, or likely to suffer significant harm. In the 1980s, social workers were

admonished to drop 'the rule of optimism' and to realise that the focus on supporting parents has often been to the detriment of the child. The very public child death enquiries often directed criticism at social workers and the poverty of information sharing within the interagency context. The dilemma for social workers is that violence towards the child's mother was a feature of a significant number of child death enquiries (O'Hara, 1994) and hence looms as a worrying issue which requires careful assessment when weighing up the risks to children in their families.

Further government initiatives which will influence statutory childcare work in the future has been provided through *Quality protects* (DoH, 1998a) and *Framework for the assessment of children in need and their families* (DoH, 1999a). *Quality protects* (DoH, 1998a) highlights a broad range of issues to improve services for children and demands tangible outcomes for the £375 million national investment over a three-year period. However, while 'listening to the views and wishes of children and young people' could be considered to be a broad objective for which local authorities could request special children's services grants, the priorities tend to favour improving services at the 'heavy end' of child protection. Local authorities, in fact, are spending 46% of the total expenditure on "Increasing the choice of adoption, foster and residential care placements for looked-after children" (DoH, 1999b). Such priorities, while extremely important, will do little to assist a shift towards resourcing greater provision for children who have not been registered through the child protection process.

The Department of Health guidance on assessment (DoH, 1999a) has sought to provide a more comprehensive framework for assessment which takes into account the broad environmental factors which may affect the care of children. The assessment is designed to be relevant to children at any stage within the referral process and to focus on the child's needs rather than incidents of abuse.

The relationship between providing assessment and services for children in need and undertaking a child protection enquiry is not straightforward. Hughes (1996) argues that the intention of the DoH reports is to rebalance the interrelationship of need and risk and not to continue developing polarity between protection and support in statutory work with children and families. While theoretically this is a useful stance, the lack of resources to fund anything but services to those children designated in the highest need categories, combined with the conservative practices which can develop when social workers live in fear of 'getting it wrong', continue to make refocusing work with children and their families an extremely difficult balancing act.

Emerging patterns

This report discusses a range of themes that emerged when case files were examined, and social workers interviewed, to explore the issues of practice in relation to domestic violence and child abuse. There is a brief methodology section (see the Appendix) which outlines the research design. A number of patterns emerged in relation to domestic violence and child protection, including the particular issues that arose for Asian families. Attention is given to the context in which child abuse occurred and looks at issues of the physical and mental health of mothers and fathers, and of alcohol abuse. A focus was also given to the intervention outcomes. These included: the accommodation of children; the strategies which focused on the domestic violence offender (usually the man); the level of attention to the child; the intervention focused on the child's mother; the legal issues; and the attention to worker safety.

This report will concentrate on two overall themes that emerged in relation to the sub-themes mentioned above, and which are particularly pertinent in the development of practice, supervision, training and policy in relation to domestic violence and child abuse. This involves an examination of the pendulum swing from *avoidance and minimisation* of the issues of domestic violence – the dominant pattern – to the smaller, though emerging, pattern of *confrontation* in which the most serious intervention strategies, including the removal of children, were now being taken.

Good practice examples are drawn out to illustrate particular themes at the beginning of most sections. Findings are then discussed in the context of other research and possible future directions for policy and practice in relation to domestic violence and child abuse.

Work with Asian and White families

The term 'Asian' is used in this report to refer to children, men and women who have an ethnic and cultural heritage which originates from the Indian sub-continent and refers to people from India, Pakistan, Bangladesh or Asian communities in Africa. It does not necessarily depict their place of birth or nationality. It thus includes children of mixed heritage. The term 'black' is used as a political term for people who suffer from racism and powerlessness. This term is used in the text where the discussion does not refer solely to the situation of Asian people. Neither term is ideal, and does not portray the full variety of backgrounds and experiences involved (Bhatti-Sinclair, 1994, p 95).

Initially, the authority had hoped that a comparative analysis could be made between work with Asian and white families to highlight where practice might be developed to become more sensitive to the needs of Asian children and their families. Stratified sampling occurred which ensured that Asian families were well represented in the research. It therefore needs to be stated clearly that the representation of Asian families in the research is due to the sampling technique which looked at every Asian family who went to a child protection conference in a two-year period from the two teams, whereas only a selected sample of white families was taken. It is therefore *not* due to a higher rate of domestic violence within that ethnic group. However, in a qualitative sample, the context and the incidents of abuse are extremely varied, making a direct comparison of the intervention between families impossible.

Case example: Family 11

An Asian family in which one of the children was badly bruised on the hand after being hit with a stick. It was unclear whether domestic violence, and the children witnessing this violence, was current or in the past. The father had mental health problems and was taking his medication very erratically.

The children were removed at the point of referral, pending an investigation. At the child protection conference there was a further recommendation for the accommodation of the children to continue pending a family assessment.

The example of Family 11 highlights the methodological issue. There was no white family in which the children were removed following a first incident of physical abuse, particularly where the mother and father were keen to cooperate with social services. However, there was also no other white family with this particular constellation of factors with which the intervention could be accurately compared.

Nevertheless, it could be argued that the negative *experience* of the intervention was compounded by the issues of racism and cultural factors (Atkar et al, 1997). Family 11 exemplifies this point. In this case, there was no Asian foster family available and the three children were not placed with another Asian family, but in a white family where there was little attention to their cultural needs. The alienation experienced at the child protection conference was increased by the need for an interpreter who in this case left the conference early to attend another appointment. There were problems arranging supervised contact with Punjabi-speaking workers. The mental health assessment for the father was delayed excessively as it was difficult to find a professional with the appropriate expertise who would undertake the assessment. This caused delay in the whole intervention process.

Family 11 was not alone in their experience of increased vulnerability to secondary trauma through the intervention process. The attention to the particular issues for Asian families will be attended to with details of their experience within the discussion of the different themes highlighted in the study.

2

Issues of physical health: the domination of 'the atrocity story'

Case example: Family 30

Mrs S has four children. She was the subject of a very violent attack from her ex-partner when she said she was leaving him. In the attack her leg was broken. This was one of six serious incidents that involved injury to the mother. She moved initially to a refuge and then to stay with an elderly aunt. Her ex-partner has been charged on two counts, one with wounding under Section 20. In spite of concerns about the harm to the children of witnessing violence towards their mother, a strategy meeting was held with the mother present, rather than a child protection conference, as this was considered to be more supportive for Mrs S. At this meeting a package of support was agreed with the mother. The social worker acted as the case coordinator and worked with the mother to organise counselling for the children, domicilary care for the mother while she was disabled with her injuries, support for rehousing, and a referral to the mental health team for assistance with her depression. A letter on file thanks the social worker for all her help and support.

There are a number of points which can be made about this case. The partnership between the social worker with Mrs S was easier than in some cases as both the worker and Mrs S were working towards the same goals: separation from the violent partner and the move to a safer more secure environment for the mother and children. The police had also taken the matter seriously and were actively pursuing serious charges against the man. The social worker recognised that supporting the mother was the most effective way of protecting the children and actively encouraged and worked with her throughout the crisis. While the lobbying from the social worker was useful in terms of housing reallocation, she had no success in arranging domiciliary care (the only part of the package that would be funded was assistance with the shopping, and that at a charge of £3.00 and only at the local store), and there were initially serious problems in gaining a referral to the mental health team. The mother's bereavement issues over the death of a previous baby and post-natal depression did not initially meet the threshold for a service. Mrs S was eventually offered mild anti-depressants and counselling which she found to be helpful and effective support at a time of crisis.

A further pertinent issue is that in this case the man's violence is named as the most serious threat to the well-being of the children and the mother is supported through the process of re-establishment to prevent the children being accommodated. She was also given a clear sense that her welfare and safety was of importance.

This attention to the issue of domestic violence was far from universal in this sample. However, where children were physically or sexually abused, or where there were severe injuries sustained by the mother, there was more likelihood that the violence would be named and considered as an issue of concern. Within this sample, 'the atrocity story' of severe physical abuse appeared to dominate responses to domestic violence while less visible forms of violence tended to be ignored.

Findings: In this study, 11 women were reported to have severe injuries as a result of incidents of domestic violence. These injuries included: two women whose legs were broken, one woman whose leg was dislocated, one woman who among other abuses was attacked around the face and who, over a period of time, experienced permanent visual impairment. The same man became involved with another woman and he continued this form of attack on the next woman. One woman was taken to hospital and treated for stab wounds, one woman bedridden for several weeks with a back injury following a violent attack, one woman's ribs were broken and she sustained severe facial bruising, and one woman's jaw was broken. One woman was scalded with boiling water. Another woman was hospitalised following severe physical neglect as a result of domestic violence and alcohol abuse, while another woman suffered a fractured nose and other injuries which required hospital treatment.

Injury and domestic violence

This study reflected other research that shows alarming levels of injury for women who are attacked by their partners or ex-partners. Other countries, such as the United States, Canada and Australia, have given considerable attention to domestic violence as a significant public health issue. This agenda has been slower to develop in Britain. Australian research estimated the cost of intentionally inflicted injuries identified in the hospital system at $286 million (approximately £143 million) per annum (*National Strategy on Violence Against Women*, 1993). Stanko et al (1998) estimated that in one London borough the overall cost of providing assistance, support and advice for domestic violence in 1996 was approximately £7.5 million. The health costs they estimated at £580,000, although this excluded hospitalisation and medicines. The *British Crime Survey* (1996) indicated that in 69% of reported incidents injury had occurred, one third of cases required medical attention, and of these 13% resulted in broken bones. Self-report questionnaires filled in anonymously by women waiting in accident and emergency departments showed that 24–35% of

women had experienced violence (Victim Support, 1992, p 20). A research study by Stark and Flitcraft (1996) showed that 9.6% of 481 women who were seen in accident and emergency departments during a one-month sample period had been assaulted by their partner, and that a further 15.4% of women had trauma histories which were indicative of domestic violence.

Injury and child protection

A number of child protection issues arise in the context of injury to the child's mother. Firstly, research suggests that men who commit serious assaults on women are highly likely to also be directly physically or sexually abusing the children. A study by Ross (1996) based on 3,363 American parents found that each additional act of violence towards the woman increased the likelihood of physical abuse to the child by 12%. At the most serious end of the scale, the research showed that the most chronically violent husbands were almost certain to be physically abusing their children. The analysis of female violence towards their male partners did not show the same dramatic relationship with child abuse. While this research does not rule out other forms of domestic violence also involving the abuse of children, it does suggest that particular vigilance towards the children is demanded where the woman has been badly injured.

Secondly, women's injuries may leave them disabled for periods of time. Wolfe et al (1985) showed in an analysis of the factors effecting children that 19% of the variance in children's behavioural problems were associated not only with witnessing domestic violence, but with maternal stress caused by maternal health problems, stressful life events and crises:

The impact on the child of witnessing wife battering may be partially a function of his or her mother's degree of impairment following such events, as well as the concomitant disruption and uncertainty the child typically faces. (Wolfe et al, 1985, p 663)

The social worker for Mrs S (mentioned above) did at least make strong (though unsuccessful) attempts to arrange domiciliary care. In other cases, women were left to make their own arrangements. The case file for Family 29, for example, records that the eldest daughter had stayed home to look after her mother whose back injury as a result of an attack had left her bedridden for two weeks. (This had not been known to the worker at the time, but had been revealed in later discussions with the child.) In other situations, the man who caused the injury may be placed in the extremely powerful position of becoming the carer for the woman on whom he has inflicted the injury. This is a doubly invidious position for disabled women who may already be dependent upon their partners either fully, or partially, for care.

Future directions in the interagency response to women's injuries

Implications arise for both social workers and other professionals responding to the needs of women and children when severe injuries occur.

Firstly, severe injuries are more easily the focus of criminal proceedings, although they are also the cases in which the extreme fear of the woman may preclude her from giving evidence. In a number of police forces, cases are now being taken forward on the basis of forensic and collaborative evidence rather than relying upon the woman as the key witness to the violence. In Case 39, forensic evidence of injury to both the mother and one of the children and the children's statements were used to take the criminal case forward in spite of the mother's withdrawal of her statement. The man was given a lengthy prison sentence as a result of the injuries he had inflicted.

Secondly, researchers have been highly critical of the health professionals' responses to domestic violence. Pahl (1995) concludes from her research with health professions that they routinely fail to identify physical abuse in women and that this reflects both the reluctance of health professionals to probe and the reluctance of women to disclose how their injuries have been caused. Similarly, Stark and Flitcraft (1996) draw a disturbing pattern of neglect by the medical profession whose interventions may not only be ineffective but can collude in shifting

blame and responsibility from the man onto the woman, who is often referred inappropriately for psychiatric treatment. Stanko et al (1998) identified GPs as a key service which women in situations of violence access, a pattern confirmed by studies of Asian women escaping domestic violence (Hendessai, 1999). Doctors are one of the few points which women find that they can legitimately and privately access, although the ability of the GP to respond to their needs was frequently reported as inadequate.

The British Medical Association (BMA) has now issued comprehensive guidelines for health workers including doctors, and a number of influential organisations have produced reports which highlight domestic violence as a health issue (SNAP, 1997; BMA, 1998). These initiatives provide some cause for optimism that work in this area may be progressing. Whether it will change such things as the attendance of GPs at child protection conferences is yet to be seen. In this sample, GPs were notable for their absence, attending only two of the conferences.

Thirdly, there are dangers in highlighting the child protection issues in cases of serious injury to women, if that is then used as an indicator of the 'woman's failure to protect' or does not galvanise a proactive response from the social worker. For instance, the social worker in Case 29 made the following comment:

"I don't think we have time to put people in touch with organisations, let alone deal with it ourselves. A good leaflet has now been put out by the police. That is about as much time as can be given to the issue. I know it sounds like a cop out."

By contrast, the social worker for Mrs S demonstrated how partnership could be developed and resources allocated to assist Mrs S through the crisis. Unfortunately, barriers were created by the lack of cooperation by health and adult services in providing a comprehensive care package when she was disabled with a broken leg. This is not a problem specific to this local authority. The SSI (Hunter, 1999) continue to highlight the dismal cooperation between these sectors, although in some local authorities the development of interface or family budgets is showing how innovative practice can work to support families where there are both adult and child protection issues (Horwath and Shardlow, forthcoming). The development of organisational policies combined with workers who have a more actively woman- and child-centred focus point to directions for future good practice.

While the attention to health problems that women face from serious assaults needs to be highlighted, both for the woman's sake as well as from the perspective of her children, there are also problems that arise if domestic violence becomes identified only with serious physical assault.

3

Falling off the agenda: minimisation and avoidance of domestic violence

Mrs L is a woman with nine children. There had been long-standing child protection concerns that culminated in a child protection conference when the 14-year-old girl in the family was referred by a third party for bruises on her arm. At the time of the conference the stepfather was considered to be 'the cornerstone of the family'. He did the washing, ironing and financially supported the family. The mother was considered to be 'not coping'. A social work student was allocated the case and at interview made the following comment:

"The problem was that no one had ever asked about domestic violence. Once the problem was named, she started to see not just the physical violence but all the subtle ways he controlled her.... She's really a different person now, but it possibly needed a social work student, who has the time, to be able to make the difference."

In this case physical violence was not often used, but the man's control through mental abuse, isolation, multiple pregnancies and undermining of the woman constituted domestic violence. The student supported the woman in naming the abuse, separating from her abusive partner, finding alternative housing and establishing a new home. At the end of the research, the case was to be closed to social work intervention, although other community links had been made.

The most common theme in the research was the minimisation of domestic violence. Unless it was a clear 'atrocity story' of violent physical assault, the issue of abuse, usually directed towards the mother, was marginalised. The stance of the social work student in naming the abuse of Mrs L in its various forms stood out as exceptional and was commented upon by her practice teacher as the difference between the dominant 'child-centred' focus of the team and the student's 'woman-centred' practice. He recognised that the latter, at least in this case, was both a more reflective practice and delivered better outcomes for the children. The minimisation of domestic violence by child protection workers is a theme commented upon by other researchers (Maynard, 1985; Milner, 1993). More specifically the ways in which power and control is established tends to be overlooked. The research pointed to a range of strategies through which social workers and other professionals avoided domestic violence.

Assessment

Firstly there are a range of micro-practices relevant to the assessment process where minimisation occurred.

The history of intervention with Family 36 is a good example of one of these micro-practices, namely *supporting the man as the cornerstone of the family*, rather than challenging his abuse. This pattern was evident in another three cases where there appeared to be consistent minimisation of the man's violence as he was seen to be more functional with the children and with the household domestic arrangements. He presented himself as the more plausible and stable parent. However, in reading through the later developments in these cases, two of the women made substantial recoveries in their mental health and support for their children when separation occurred.

A related issue, and a factor in the process of minimisation, was *to name the mother's violence as more of, or as great a, problem as the man's violence* towards her. In one situation where both parents had moderate learning difficulties and few social skills, this was possibly an accurate assessment as violent acts seemed to be attributable to both parties and both had been involved in incidents with other people (Family 27). However, other assessments colluded with the man's violence and definition of the situation (Families 22, 35, 37). This is a particular problem for social workers who are often untrained in work with offenders. They are easily invited into 'the responsibility vacuum' created by offenders who are able to rationalise most forms of violence: any act of resistance is construed as provocation, and denial is their main form of defense (Jenkins, 1989).

Case example: Family 22

Mr K is an Asian man married to Mrs K, a white woman who he became involved with when she was a teenager. They now have six children. The social work report to the child protection conference concluded that domestic violence occurred when the mother was drunk and attacked her partner. In self-defense, or out of frustration with her, he then retaliated. The woman agreed that this was how violence was instigated.

However, this construction of the family dynamics ignored a range of issues documented at other times in the case file. These were namely that: the husband was extremely controlling; he refused to move from a two-bedroomed house where he ran a small business to a four-bedroomed house which was available for his family of six children; his wife was kept constantly pregnant and not allowed to use birth control; she was isolated, with no phone; she was not allowed to visit her family; her attempts to gain control

of her alcohol problem were undermined by him; and he had assaulted her so seriously that the police have been called – these assaults had occurred over a 10-year period.

The social worker made a number of comments about intervening effectively with this family and on the construction of violence in the report to the child protection conference:

"The report might be construed that way. He is extremely controlling and when I work with them, I try and keep that on the agenda. He often won't even let her talk.... On the other hand, I take a systemic approach, and they both agree that is how the violence starts.... I can see that maybe it is more complex than that.... It is also difficult when he is an Asian man to be respectful of his background and values ... there is racism from the mother's family as well, although admittedly he did severely physically abuse their grandchild...."

This case highlights the complexity of assessment by a white female worker in a family with an Asian father and white mother. While the issues of cultural background and racism were significant for the father, they were also used to increase his control over, and isolation of, the mother and the children.

A further issue was *the man's lack of involvement in assessments*. Eight families were in assessment centres during the time when their file was reviewed. Only in one situation did the man stay at the centre, and in this case, both he and his partner were eventually evicted and their children accommodated in a foster family (Family 4). Some men did participate in assessment by turning up at sessions with workers, although they refused to live in the residential setting. Other men evaded any participation in the programme, but maintained a visiting relationship or resumed their relationship when the women and children left the centre. When a key issue is often his violence towards the woman, and/or children, then the evasion by men of the assessment process brings into question the usefulness of residential assessment under these circumstances.

A further issue to be discussed in the next chapter will be *the shifting of the focus of assessment* from domestic violence onto issues of mental health, alcohol abuse and child neglect. All these issues tended to place the focus on the mother's behaviour and failings and away from the offender's violence.

Reporting

There were also micro practices in relation to the files and reporting that led to the invisibility of domestic violence.

Reports failed to mention domestic violence as a relevant issue. Frequently, the social work case notes cited incidents of violence towards the mother, but these were then not written into reports to child protection conferences, assessment reports or the file case summaries. Through this process the man's offending became invisible. Social workers made comments such as:

> "I didn't think that it was relevant for the report as it did not involve the children directly. I took a different attitude when S was hit." (Family 6)

> "I must confess I haven't had time to read the whole file, so didn't know it was an issue at the time." (Family 25)

Case example: Family 35

The original referral to social services occurred following the separation of Mrs C from the children's father due to the same reason – these incidents were mentioned in the social work file notes but never as formal reports. A list of nine hazards listed for this family does not identify the father's violence to Mrs C. The report to the child protection conference failed to mention that the woman had been assaulted and her house 'trashed' only a few days prior to the report for the child protection conference being written. One of the three children was in the house at the time. In the interview with the social worker, she remembered the incident clearly as she had been shocked at the time at the level of damage that she saw when she had visited the flat – furniture had been ripped apart with a knife. She said:

> "I can't imagine why it is not in the report.... I can only think that I didn't think it is the type of thing that is relevant to the child protection conference, particularly in making decisions about care proceedings. They're not interested in domestic violence."

Family 16 provides a further illustration of the problem. The conference chair (in an adjoining local authority) provided a case summary in which he acknowledged that the mother's depression was understandable: "in the short space of four months she has had a traumatic birth, followed by the tragic accident of her brother and she has moved into an area where she is isolated and unsupported". This summary somewhat underplays the fact that she has been assaulted a number of times during her pregnancy and following the birth of her child in incidents serious enough to call the police, and that the man at the very least was sexually overly demanding if not sexually assaulting the woman, pressuring her for sex against her wishes on a daily basis since the birth of her baby. While the chair's summary might have assisted in the active engagement of the man who was present, it did little to name one of the core problems in the family.

Evidence also existed of changes in attitudes over time. In one long-standing case, a social work report from 1988 documents evidence of the mother's drinking and neglect, but fails to mention that the father attacked the mother so violently that she was hospitalised four times. The assessment from the family centre documents the worrying effects of neglect from inconsistent care. A further stay at an assessment centre in 1993-94 at least acknowledges domestic violence as a problem as well as the alcohol abuse, although joint counselling appears to be a key (and one would suggest inappropriate) intervention offered. In 1994, when the mother reported being raped and had evidence of bruising on her shoulders and neck, she is treated sympathetically and referred appropriately for post-abuse counselling.

A further strategy which renders domestic violence invisible is *the language of minimisation* used at conferences and in reports. Examples abound in the files of instances where domestic violence is reported but not named.

One chair refers to 'an argument between the parents', which on closer reading of the file shows that the argument was actually a knife attack, resulting in the woman being stabbed by her partner. In Family 38 the conference report refers to the mother and children leaving home because of 'marital disruption'. A closer reading of the file revealed that this Asian woman and children had been forced to sit in the dark, the woman had been assaulted, and the husband tried to prevent her taking her medication. Another situation reports an Asian family (Family 13) where 'the home situation has deteriorated'. Although the social worker had interviewed both parents, she reported the view of the father who attributed 'the deterioration' to lack of employment and his wife's mental health. His response was to drink, which led to further arguments including an occasion when his wife called the police. Again, it appears likely that the police would be called where violence is threatened or occurring, *not* where there is 'an argument'. The explanation is clearly the man's and lacks the woman's perspective on the 'deterioration in the home situation'.

In summary, a range of strategies were identified through which domestic violence could be avoided by child protection workers at any stage within the process of referral, investigation and assessment. These traps can render practice ineffectual as core issues which affect the family's functioning are ignored.

Moving domestic violence onto the agenda

More recently, a number of strategies have been developed to counteract the tendency for domestic violence to become invisible. Several local authorities have developed mechanisms for *screening and monitoring* for domestic violence. Research has shown that when children and family workers proactively ask about domestic violence that twice as many cases in which violence features may come

to light (Farmer and Owen, 1995; Hester and Pearson, 1998). In some areas a code which registers cases of domestic violence is introduced into the assessment or referral form, while in other areas a monitoring form has been introduced. The use of domestic violence as a registration category is regarded as counter-productive as it may heighten women's fears of reporting without necessarily increasing support and resources (Parkinson and Humphreys, 1998).

Specialist training in the relationship between domestic violence and child abuse, including in the areas of assessment, work with black and Asian families, direct work, and mental health issues all heighten the awareness of the impact of domestic violence and prevent it from slipping to the margin in the work with children and families. The reader and training pack *Making an impact* have made a significant contribution to the training agenda (see Hester et al, 1999).

The *development of procedures and protocols* for both interagency working and work within specific organisations has also been helpful in providing clearer guidelines for workers, again heightening the importance of domestic violence as an issue of relevance and concern (see, for example, Leeds Interagency Guidelines; *Cheshire Interagency Practice Guidelines Regarding Child Protection and Domestic Violence*, 1998).

An area which needs particular attention is the relationship between services for children and services for adults within and between social services departments and health trusts.

4

Adult mental health issues: shifting or ignoring the problem

Case example: Family 5

Mrs M is an Asian woman with three children. Mr M is currently unemployed and has developed a drinking problem. There is a long history of violence by Mr M towards his wife. The police have had to be called to the house on many occasions. The case conference has been called following concerns about Mr M's 'rough playing' with the three children, the last episode leaving the oldest child with a bite mark on her arm. Mrs M has had mental health problems in the past. The report for conference states that these are attributed to fears created by Jehovah's Witnesses and her husband's violence and drinking.

The report for Family 5 is exceptional in drawing the link between the husband's violence and the woman's mental health problems. Generally, this sample showed high overall rates of mental health problems, particularly for the women. However, these problems were given little attention unless they were seen to directly affect child protection issues. Little connection was made between mental health issues for women and domestic violence.

Findings: in this sample of 32 cases there were three men cited with mental health problems and 13 women.

Mental health issues for men

The three men cited in the sample were Asian men. One man was diagnosed with schizophrenia, one with severe mood swings which had led to previous hospitalisation and medication, and one with depression with associated paranoid symptoms.

The intervention in two of the families where physical violence to children and domestic violence occurred in the context of the man's mental health problems highlighted major problems in joint working arrangements between adult and children's teams. These issues were compounded by the problem of gaining appropriate mental health assessments for Asian men. The consequences of this fragmentation were extreme for both these families where the men had been explicitly told at child protection conferences that they must leave the family while an assessment was undertaken. Failure to comply would lead to the accommodation of the children.

Family 11 (discussed earlier, see p 5) complied with child protection conference recommendations, and the man left the family to stay, at least initially, with his father. However, the delays associated with gaining a mental health assessment for this man were extreme. His mental and physical health deteriorated during this delay and he died of a heart attack at age 33.

Case example: Family 38

Mr S's behaviour had been increasingly threatening towards his wife and three children since he had been taking medication erratically. He was sectioned under the Mental Health Act (1983) for assessment within a hospital setting. In the meantime, work was to be undertaken with the mother and children. The child protection conference recommended that, "should Mr S return to the family the children would be accommodated" Unfortunately, the hospital appeared to want to 'clear beds' prior to Christmas, and in spite of the protestation from the children and family social worker, and although no substantial mental health assessment had been undertaken, Mr S was discharged. Mrs S was told that under the circumstances she must leave home with the children or else the children would be accommodated. She and the children moved into completely inappropriate hostel rooms over the Christmas period. She has since returned home. Over two months after the child protection conference recommendation for an assessment of the mental health and cultural issues for the father, an assessment had still not commenced. Prior to the 'Christmas debacle', Mrs S had had good relations with social services. However, she has since become mistrusting, Mr S's power has been increased, and Mrs S and the children have become more isolated from any outside support.

Again, the intervention in this case highlights the problems created for both workers and families when there is no joint planning between professionals.

In both these mental health assessments for Asian men, the issues appeared to be complicated by the confusion workers felt there was between the role of soothsayers, religious practices and psychosis. Moreover, interpreters were rarely used by community psychiatric nurses or on hospital ward rounds, in spite of the need for this resource in both these cases. The issue of violence towards their wives was given no attention, though it has to be said that as one man died before he had an

assessment, and the other man was sent home prior to any assessment occurring, that domestic violence was not the only issue which was ignored.

Mental health issues for women

Mental health issues were cited for women in 13 of the 32 cases. With two exceptions these issues were avoided. Generally, no connection was made between depression or psychosis and domestic violence, although on three occasions it was mentioned in notes or reports that there was a significant improvement in the mother's mental health following separation from her violent partner.

When mental health problems occurred in the context of the mother's alcohol abuse, the mental health problems were given no attention. Phobic and anxiety states (present in three cases) in the context of alcohol abuse are mentioned in passing, but are not followed up in the case plan or seen as worthy of further intervention. There appeared to be a significant minimisation of the relationship between mental health problems, particularly depression, and domestic violence. The extent of impairment and the sources of depression appear often to be unexplored. An exception lay with the social worker for Family 30 (mentioned earlier, see p 7), who provided holistic support for a woman by attending to her housing, domiciliary and psychological needs. This included counselling and the prescription by the woman's GP of a mild anti-depressant which she took to good effect.

Of the 12 Asian families in which domestic violence was an issue, five women were reported with mental health problems. The issues of finding appropriate help and sensitive mental health assessments which probe the issues of domestic violence are compounded where there are issues of language barriers, community isolation and migration status (Ingram, 1993; Newham Asian Women's Project, 1995). For example, Mrs S (Family 38 mentioned earlier, p 15) had also been diagnosed with schizophrenia. She was taking approximately three times the medication of her husband, yet the onset of the psychosis was closely associated with the beginning of violence from her husband and the birth of her second child. There had been no recent reassessment of her situation and her medication and the links with domestic violence had not been made.

Studies of women and mental health illustrate the serious impact of domestic violence. Jacobson and Richardson (1987) showed that 60-70% of women in one mental health unit had been abused. Research by Stark (1984) indicated that 25% of women admitted for emergency psychiatric care had experienced domestic violence. These are similar figures to a study by Tham et al (1995) which shows 24% of 184 patients screened over a five-month period in an adult psychiatric service were victims of domestic violence. Other studies have identified the high correlation between women's suicide attempts and their experience of assault from their partner or ex-partner. Sixty-five per cent of women had been assaulted within six months of their first suicide attempt (Stark and Flitcraft, 1996). However, mental health services frequently ignore the violence that may be the precursor to the woman's suicide attempts or psychological problems (Orr, 1984; Gelles and Harrop, 1989).

There has also recently been work undertaken on the links between mental health, child abuse and domestic violence. Stanley and Penhale (1999) point out that all 13 women in their study of children at risk of significant harm whose mothers were suffering from severe mental health problems were also all the subject of domestic violence. However, the children's problems were raised in relation to the mother's mental health, not the father's violence. They also point out that six of the women in the study were labelled as having 'personality disorder'. This category is often used to preclude people from services, and identifies them as 'management problems', placing the responsibility back onto the service user and away from the professionals (Grounds, 1995). It is the pattern noted also by Kurz and Stark (1988) who identified how the intervention of the medical profession progressively named the woman as the problem and identified her symptoms as the cause rather than the consequence of the violence she experienced.

The numbers of women in this study suffering from impaired mental health, particularly where domestic violence was an issue, suggest that child protection workers need to give this issue much greater consideration. Women with mental health issues are considerably hampered in their ability to look after their children, and the source of these substantial problems may well lie in the violence they experience from their partners. This was an issue which in these cases was not adequately explored in either investigations or assessments.

Future directions

Work is now developing to overcome the barriers between health and social services. The government has committed itself to initiatives which will enhance this process with the development of Primary Care Groups and pilot schemes in which mental health services are provided by joint health and social service teams. There are also a number of joint training initiatives (Diggins and Mazey, 1998) and strategy meetings between managers of adult mental health teams and children's and families' teams. On the agenda for management are the problematic issues of *different thresholds* for referral, assessment and intervention support, and specifying interface or *family budgets* to avoid the unhelpful 'buck passing' between teams. Currently there may be problems about who will fund the package of care for the family where there are both adult problems and child abuse problems. Creating the links between teams at management level is being undertaken in some areas to facilitate a more holistic approach to families.

Joint working is also occurring in some areas, with a worker from an adult team and a worker from a children's and families' team undertaking assessments and investigations together. A worker focused on the adult's needs and another focused on the children provides a significant bridge for this work, particularly where domestic violence is an issue. It is also a strategy for overcoming frustrating problems of fragmentation in which children's and families' workers become distressed by the lack of attention to the child protection needs in the mental health assessment, or alternatively are incensed by the recommendations of psychiatrists about childcare issues when they may not have interviewed or observed the children with their parents.

This research also highlights the particular
difficulties which may arise in gaining mental health
assessments sensitive to cross-cultural issues. The
lack of expertise in this area by psychiatrists led to
unacceptably long delays, lack of intervention and
an overuse of drugs. Innovative work is now being
undertaken in areas such as Newham where a
mental health project runs alongside the Asian
Women's Support Service, while in other areas black
psychiatrists have consistently pushed for more
appropriate resources, services and assessments for
ethnic minority populations (Sashidaran, 1989).

A further area for exploration lies with
interventions where domestic violence and alcohol
abuse are linked – an area in which similar themes
in relation to child protection and adult services
arise.

5

Alcohol abuse: a brewing problem in domestic violence

Mrs M is an Asian woman with three children whose husband is violent towards her, particularly when he is under the influence of alcohol. The intervention focused on his alcohol abuse rather than violence. However, it was not a simple matter of 'slipping away' from the issue of violence. The social worker made the following comment:

"In some ways I took the lead from Mrs M who felt that if the drinking could be stopped, the violence would not be a problem.... She could be very direct with him about the drinking because I think she had the support of her family and the mosque ... the violence was more of a problem in that respect ... she had less support there."

The dilemmas in working with the link between domestic violence and alcohol or drug abuse pose particular problems for intervention in this area.

There is a well documented association between alcohol abuse and domestic violence (Gelles, 1993; Conner and Ackerley, 1994). However, researchers and women working in the field also stress that the relationship is not causal and that in fact the large majority of batterers have battered while sober or following only moderate drinking (Sonkin, 1985; Eberle, 1982). Gelles (1993) in an overview article of the research on the association between alcohol abuse and domestic violence argues that there is little causal evidence for this link. However, he cites the work of MacAndrew and Edgerton (1969), which has been further developed by Lang et al (1975), suggesting that in our society when people drink or believe they are drunk, they are given 'time out' from the normal rules of social behaviour. Thus, perpetrators who wish to avoid responsibility can do so by drinking before they are violent, or at least by saying they were drunk.

Men and alcohol abuse

In 18 of the 32 cases alcohol abuse by the mother's partner is named as a problem. Domestic violence frequently occurred in the context of alcohol abuse and thus constitutes a significant pattern in this sample.

A number of issues emerged:

- There was a general failure for the men to take responsibility for their alcohol abuse.
- Within the context of child protection issues, it appeared to be easier for a child protection conference to name and tackle the man's alcohol abuse rather than domestic violence. Hence the problem was frequently named as the man's alcohol abuse, not domestic violence. Assessments were often framed 'to look at Mr X's alcohol abuse' rather than 'explore the nature and effects of Mr X's domestic violence on his wife and children'. Or if the child protection conference had named the domestic violence, the assessment may have concentrated on alcohol abuse, so that in the report or work which is undertaken, the issue of domestic violence is lost.
- The ability to gain some leverage in the situation, with the exception of one man, only occurred in

this sample following jail and/or probation orders. There were five cases in which men had been jailed and on release showed some compliance with attendance at alcohol advisory services.

The exception involved sustained work over eight months with a social worker who managed to engage the man in the work and tackle some of the dynamics which created vulnerabilities for the woman and children in the family.

Women and alcohol abuse

In seven cases the mother's alcohol or drug abuse is named as a problem.

Again, a number of patterns emerged.

- Frequently, the focus of the child protection inquiry became the mother's alcohol abuse. Clearly at times this was of major significance. Nevertheless, the important relationship between alcohol abuse by women and the domestic violence that they suffered was not recognised. Three out of the seven women returned to drinking which they had under total or some control following a violent attack by their partners. At other times, men rationalised violence towards their partners on the basis that the woman was drinking. Such patterns of behaviour are confirmed by the research by Fagan et al (1988) who found that women were more vulnerable to being battered on occasions when they drank. The three reported attacks by women on their partners also appeared to occur in the context of her drinking.
- By the time some of these families came to the notice of social services, domestic violence had occurred over many years, and the key problem within the family was now named as the mother's abuse of alcohol. Two women began to gain some control over their alcoholism when they separated from their partners and other members of the family who were drinking. One of these women was greatly assisted by the work she undertook with the child protection social worker.
- At times there appears to be an overly optimistic approach to managing the problems of alcohol

abuse. One mother incinerated the house when drunk, almost killing her children. All plans at rehabilitation of the children were suspended. However, within two months rehabilitation to the mother was being reconsidered by the child protection conference as she had had a short period of abstinence and appeared to have a new male partner. Such decisions can be extremely disruptive in the lives of children.

In this sample the issues of drug abuse were minimal relative to that of alcohol abuse.

Future directions

Issues of alcohol abuse have always been a 'brewing problem' in the area of domestic violence. It consistently provides the easiest rationalisation for violence and abuse and the simplest diversion from the problem. Offender programmes have generally been appropriately cynical about this diversion, and while recognising there is sometimes an association between alcohol abuse and domestic violence, will use the group process to explore further the man's distorted thinking in relation to alcohol and violence. However, alcohol services have traditionally been less confronting about this issue, not necessarily by condoning violence, but by failing to ask the questions which would elicit the story of the man's violence.

Domestic violence training in the area of alcohol abuse is potentially bringing a shift in practice. However, it is an issue that requires skilled intervention. Alcohol services are one of the few counselling/education services with which men will voluntarily engage (though this was not evidenced in this particular sample). It is therefore crucial that relatively crude and ineffective 'confrontation methods' aimed at 'breaking down the man's defenses' are not the first method of choice – a problem if the issue is taken up by workers who have only been engaged in awareness-raising training, without a further development in specialist skills. Asking questions about men's violence and abuse in ways that build aspects of their motivation and self-worth through the work is a skilled process (Jenkins, 1989), but one which will need to be developed if men are to appropriately take responsibility for their violence and alcohol abuse.

Early intervention and drawing the connections between women's alcohol problems and domestic violence needs to be explored in assessments and work with women in this area. The developing links between children's services and adult alcohol services is one which has been commented upon favourably in a recent SSI report (Hunter, 1999). Such links create potential for appropriate service provision in the area.

Alcohol abuse by Asian men was a significant problem in the sample of Asian families and suggests that specialist Asian workers are a much-needed resource in this area.

This sample suggested that significant leverage can be achieved to work with violent men on their issues to do with violence and alcohol abuse if they have been arrested, convicted and are in the community on license or probation orders. This work may only be short-term, but it could be the only time in which any work is undertaken which is focused on men taking responsibility for their abuse.

In short, the connections between alcohol abuse and domestic violence are complex when the issue of intervention is considered. Engaging men about their alcohol abuse has traditionally been easier than engaging them about their violence. Shifting the focus so that domestic violence is no longer 'off the agenda' is not straightforward and requires skilled intervention and support within the interagency network.

The process in relation to tackling violence and alcohol abuse highlights the broader issue of engaging men in statutory childcare work. This is a complex area which requires more detailed consideration.

6

Focusing on offenders: 'challenging the invisible man'

Case example: Family 39

Mr L has a series of convictions for violence over a period of 15 years. In the latest incident bought to this child protection conference, Mr L had attacked the mother and children when he was drunk. This involved a serious assault in which Mr L repeatedly crashed one of the children down on a piece of furniture, injuring the child. He also attacked the mother when she was trying to leave. In the process he kicked and punched the pregnant mother in the stomach and dislocated her leg. Mr L was charged over the incident and was jailed as he was already on bail for affray. Following the child protection conference, the mother worked closely with the social worker, who assisted with both practical and emotional issues but was unable to organise appropriate rehousing. Prior to the court case the mother dropped the charges and said she would not attend the court. The police nevertheless pressed ahead with the case on the basis of the forensic and medical evidence from both the children and mother. Mr L was convicted and jailed.

The proactive response from the police in this case through gathering the evidence and placing it before the court meant that criminal action was taken on the assaults and the mother was not placed in the situation of giving evidence against a man who terrified her.

Shifting the focus of child protection onto the man and his violence provides a continuing challenge to each of the professionals involved where domestic violence is an issue. The tendency to focus on the mother, her problems and her 'failure to protect' is an altogether too familiar pattern in child welfare work (Milner, 1993). Child and family social workers and health visitors in particular tend to work primarily with women and are rarely trained to engage men in their work. Conversely, men frequently slip away from either support or scrutiny by statutory workers, leaving the mother 'holding the baby'. In this process, the man and his violence may become invisible.

Other studies of statutory childcare work by Maynard (1985), Milner (1993) and Farmer (1997) have documented this pattern. Farmer's (1997) research on child protection files showed that the mother's physical abuse of children was taken much more seriously. She makes the following comment:

Moreover, when a man's physical abuse of a child had led to registration, it was a matter of considerable concern to find that the attention of professionals quickly moved away from the man and came to rest on the mother, who was seen as more amenable to intervention. (Farmer 1997, p 159)

The Coventry research showed a similar pattern of scrutinising the mother's behaviour, rather than the man's violence, although later files (1995/96) showed that the child protection conference made more discernible attempts to focus on the man. These efforts met with greater or lesser success, and generally highlighted the lack of development in practice with men.

Recommendations which potentially involved the man included:

- Four recommendations that the man was not to return home until an assessment had been undertaken, without any legal framework in the form of injunctions, probation orders or bail conditions for enforcing such a recommendation. Two of the four men 'complied' in so far as they did not return to the home, although there were significant complications for the woman and children involved in one case.

- Four assessments prior to the man returning home which were in the context of probation or bail conditions (all men complied to some degree).

- Two letters inviting the man to attend an interview with the social worker (not taken up).

- One expensive counselling package for an extremely violent man who had never been arrested for any of the offences which he had perpetrated (not taken up).

- Seven comprehensive assessments in the home, most of which specified both parents and did not necessarily mention the issue of domestic violence as a focus for assessment. Potentially, these assessments could have addressed the issue of domestic violence.

Clearly, approximately half the sample had no child protection intervention which even potentially addressed the man's violence. The most useful were strategies that occurred within a legal framework, while the evidence from this sample showed that most other attempts were ineffective.

Legal responses

Civil orders

Women were often advised by conferences and the Police Domestic Violence Liaison Unit to take out injunctions against their partners or ex-partners. This research was undertaken prior to the Family Law Act (1996) and at least four of the women had significant problems gaining injunctions with powers of arrest. One of the women who had an undertaking was told by the police that it was useless and advised her to return to court. In another case an offender convinced the court that

there were no further problems (at the same time threatening the woman "that grassers should be shot").

While non-molestation orders and occupation orders without power of arrest are now less of a problem, the courage required to take out non-molestation orders against partners and ex-partners needs to be recognised. Women in this sample who did not have English as a first language, who had learning difficulties and mental health problems, were being advised at child protection conferences to take these steps, but without a worker necessarily designated by the conference to assist with the safety planning and advocacy involved. Research has consistently highlighted the particular problems for Asian women in seeking legal remedies and using the courts to address violence from their partners (Choudry, 1996; Bhatti-Sinclair, 1994). Such evidence points to the need for proactive and sensitive support if women are to access the legal system. At the very least, recommendations from child protection conferences should be given in evidence at these hearings for non-molestation orders and occupation orders, particularly if the child protection conference recommendation is that the children are to be accommodated if the man returns home.

Criminal proceedings

In this sample, eight men had been charged with serious offences which meant that they were either in jail, on probation, or released early on license. Two of the men were charged with offences directly related to domestic violence, although one of these charges (Family 3) could be seen as racist. The six other men were on other charges, although sometimes the incident of domestic violence had occurred while on bail or probation, and the domestic violence led to a breach and subsequent jail sentence. In these circumstances there is much more 'leverage' to put demands and strictures on the behaviour of these men. On several occasions police, quite appropriately, wrote bail conditions which placed an exclusion zone around the home and denied contact and access to the women and children.

Given the level of violence experienced by many of the women in the group, the rate of arrest of men for assaults on women remains low, an issue which is commented upon in most reports on domestic violence (Barron, 1990; Grace, 1995). Frequently, in these situations police say that there is not enough evidence on which to arrest a man. Yet one Asian man was arrested and held in custody for two weeks pending the court case, in spite of the woman having no discernible marks of the assault by the time of the medical (only a few hours after reporting) and the child similarly suffered only minor bruising. One might suggest that such proactive policing was evidence of good practice. It allowed space for the woman and children to consider their futures, and it gave a short, sharp shock for the man who was then amenable to work with probation and alcohol advisory services. During assessment, he undertook work with social workers on improving his relationship with the children. Many white women may have benefited from similar proactive policing. However, the fact that no other man in the sample was treated in this way suggests that the police were much more interested in attempting to deport the man under the one-year rule, and as such this constitutes evidence of racism rather than good practice, an issue clearly articulated by Mama (1989) in relation to domestic violence and statutory institutions.

In this sample, men who were on probation, or released on license, were more amenable to referral to alcohol advisory services, group work for men who are violent, and assessment procedures from social workers. At the very least, these demands allowed the woman and children some 'abuse free' time, some potential for the men to gain help should they want it, and placed the onus of responsibility on the men. Child protection conferences which do not make these recommendations miss important opportunities for offender-focused work. Two men were still in jail at the time of the study, two of the eight conferences missed these opportunities to make recommendations associated with probation orders or bail conditions.

It has to be said however that the cooperation was not long lasting. Of the six men released from jail, four had re-offended by the end of the research period. In this sample, the 'new, reformed men' fresh from jail or on probation and involved in alcohol or short-term 'anger management groups'

(no men were involved in a sustained group work programme to address the man's violence) only seemed to last the distance while they were on probation or free on license.

In summary, the measures which were taken with the men in most cases did not prove particularly effective in preventing further incidents of violence. I suspect that a couple of women would say that some of the intervention has had some effect in so far as the violence has become more intermittent or ceased for a period of time, and that they have experienced some greater compliance from their partners over some situations. (It would require further research to follow up this issue.) In one situation where a man was on a probation order, effective long-term work appears to have been undertaken and the violence has ceased (Family 23). In another situation (Family 24) there was a serious incident of violence. However, following a separation, long-term work with this family has continued and the mother and father continue to work well with the social worker to look at the issues of rehabilitation of the children from foster placements back to the family. Other situations escalated. Generally the pressure remains on the woman to separate if the violence is to cease.

Future directions

Strategies which hold the man responsible for his violence are not only the concern of social workers, but a part of a wider interagency responsibility. The crime reduction strategy in each regional area is creating greater impetus to deal with the policing of domestic violence in some areas. This research highlighted the fact that it was easier for child protection workers to tackle domestic violence offenders if the police had taken the issue seriously through charging, arrest and the application of appropriate and protective bail conditions.

The police project in the Killingbeck Division of West Yorkshire suggests that active policing which presents a consistent approach to offenders provides a helpful framework for intervention (Hanmer et al, 1999). Women reported that arrest and charging was effective, particularly where the man had 'something to lose' either in terms of respect within the family or in relation to his work; that letters to offenders which told them that police surveillance would continue were experienced as supportive; and that a police watch where police cars could be seen patrolling made women feel less isolated. Consistency in relation to breaching offenders was also an essential ingredient to restraining domestic violence offenders.

Other areas are implementing either fully or partially the Duluth Model's approach to offenders (Pense, 1987). Hammersmith and Fulham epitomises the approach and is working towards a comprehensive interagency approach to domestic violence which will be underpinned by proactive policing and supportive outreach strategies towards women in crisis. The Domestic Violence Intervention Project (Burton et al, 1998) provides a high-quality offender programme based on a re-education model and parallel women's project and is an integral part of the strategy. Other areas are providing not only women's groups, but children's groups running alongside offender programmes. The pursuit of so-called 'victimless prosecutions' described at the outset of this section (Family 39) is a further example of proactive policing which can make a considerable difference to the protection of both women and children.

However, while active policing is an important backdrop to child welfare and child protection intervention, it does not alleviate the responsibility for social workers to shift the focus of their work where domestic violence is an issue. Sometimes this will mean working directly with offenders, other times it will imply sympathetically working with the woman to attend to the abuse she is experiencing in tandem with attending to the issues for the child.

A number of issues are pertinent when shifting the focus to the offender.

- Greater attention will need to be given to the assessment of offenders. While one can hope that children will be bought up safely and non-violently, the thresholds of safety need to be evaluated and will often need to be undertaken in safety planning with the mother, so that if precipitative action is being considered thoughtful assessment occurs. There are indicators of danger which need to be considered. These could include: the presence of guns (increases risk eight times); previous use of weapons; threats with weapons; threats to kill; previous serious injury; threats of suicide; drug or alcohol misuse; forced sex; obsessiveness/extreme jealousy (from Campbell, 1995); depression; repeated intervention by law enforcement; escalation of risk taking; separation; hostage taking; and physical and sexual abuse of children alongside the abuse of the child's mother. The more indicators that are present, the greater the risk and the greater the need for support, advocacy and intervention.

- There needs to be an assessment of the potential of the offender to change (see Burke, 1999).

- Social workers should increase joint work with police and probation officers when interviewing offenders.

- Social workers should undertake training about working with men who are violent with due consideration for safety, ongoing supervision, and setting a context for interviewing which does not increase the danger to women and children.

- Priority should be given to strategies which create alliances with women through advocacy and safety planning and which examine the range of ways in which protection for the woman and children can be enhanced.

- There needs to be recognition of the fact that separation is not only extremely difficult, but is also a time of increased risk for women and children. They will therefore need greater support and assistance at this time. Moreover, if the man is placed in custody or jailed, this provides an important opportunity for women to reassess the direction of their lives freer from control and manipulation through violence and abuse. This is a period when sustained work should be attempted, not a period of withdrawal. In this sample, child protection workers often withdrew when men were in jail as the children were seen to be 'safe'.

- Exclusion orders (Children Act Section 38 and Section 44) are now available which allow the court to exclude someone from the home who is suspected of abusing the child within the home where an emergency protection order or interim order is in place. While their use is limited to situations in which children are on the point of being accommodated, this occurred in a number of cases in this sample. Good practice potentially would lie in taking an emergency protection order and then allowing the exclusion order to be made. Four of the women in this sample were told at child protection conferences that children would be accommodated if the man returned. In these situations where the mother is also the subject of abuse, and for a range of reasons not feeling able to take her own legal protection, then a 'no-order principle' may be inappropriate. Taking action which allows the woman and children to stay in the home with legal protection is a more realistic way forward.

- The situation would be eased if Section 60 of the Family Law Act Part IV is implemented. This allows police and other authorised professionals to take out civil protection orders on behalf of the woman with her permission. This is a practice developed in Australia and New Zealand with some success (see Humphreys and Kaye, 1997). While this action is not a panacea, it would have the effect of naming the abuser's actions and providing greater legal leverage. This is particularly the case where the man is absenting himself from proceedings and therefore at this stage often beyond the reach of professionals other than through his partner.

- The notion of partnership may need to be re-considered where domestic violence is present. Joint interviews with both parents may only place the woman in danger, or lead to poor and inaccurate information. This is a particular issue in investigation, assessment and on-going work with the family. This does not imply that the man should be marginalised in the interview process, but rather that separate interviews will need to be undertaken.

In short, there are serious problems for child protection practice if an increase in attention to the relationship between child abuse and domestic violence does not bring with it a shift in practice. The 'invisible man' will need to be 're-dressed'[1] so that his actions and the effect of his behaviour on those around him is acknowledged. While women need to continue to reflect on, and address, abusive actions towards their children where this is an issue, slipping the responsibility for *domestic violence* onto the woman by focusing on her vulnerabilities and 'failure to protect' colludes with the man's violence in ways which are both unhelpful and inappropriate.

Note

[1] Chris Burke, an Australian practitioner, coined this phrase. See Burke (1999).

7

Key forums: child protection conferences and core reviews

Case example: Family 6

Mrs S is an Asian woman with seven children. Social services have been involved with the family for many years. The issues of domestic violence were considered secondary to the issues of child neglect and the mother's failure to manage the children. When the father physically abused the eldest daughter his abuse was named and recommendations were made at the child protection conference for him to live separately from the family. Given the difficulties (and expense) of sensitively accommodating such a large group of Asian children, considerable support has been provided by social services to avoid taking the step of removal. A family aide was provided on a long-term basis. The most recent social worker made a concerted effort to provide a significantly better living environment for the mother and children through gaining grants from charities and insisting that the Housing Department repair and maintain the house. In partnership with the mother, an audit of her welfare rights was undertaken and her benefits increased. The family finances have been reorganised. The father's separation from the family, combined with the partnership with the mother by both the social worker and family aide, significantly increased the mother's self-esteem. The severe emotional problems which had been previously evident in two of the children receded. The threat of accommodation is no longer imminent.

The active and very practical work by the social worker currently involved with this family provided a route to a respectful relationship with Mrs S who greatly appreciated the change in her environment and financial situation. The family aide commented that much of the previous work with this family (including her own) had been very destructive, with the mother being 'ordered around' in ways which significantly undermined her already fragile self-esteem. The current combination of respect, resources and the removal of the father, who had previously been seen to be 'the more functional parent', contributed to a new and more sustainable family unit.

Not all families in this sample faired so well.

Accommodating children: threats and realities

In this sample, *16 (50%) families had children who were accommodated by the local authority* or, in the case of an older child, privately accommodated. This involved 41 children who spent periods of time in voluntary placement or short placements on Emergency Protection Orders (EPOs), through to children being freed for adoption. *In another eight cases, mothers were warned at a strategy meeting or case conferences that if the man returned "the children would be accommodated, an EPO made, or [there would be] an immediate return to conference at which decisions would be made about the future of the children".*

Thus in this sample of 32 cases, two thirds of the women (24) were either 'threatened' with the accommodation of their children or did in fact have their children accommodated in situations where they were also the subject of abuse from violent men.

It has to be said that social workers in the study were shocked at this emerging pattern in the research. They would say that accommodation of children was always a final option after all avenues had been exhausted and that this pattern in no way represented an over-willingness to accommodate children. Certainly, reading through the files, one wondered in some (though not all) situations how extreme the situation had to become before children were accommodated. For example, in Family 4 mentioned earlier (p 20) Mrs G, whose very violent partner had died, remained with a legacy of a severe alcohol problem. She incinerated the house when drunk, almost killing her children. However, within two months, rehabilitation was reconsidered by the conference as she had had a short period of abstinence from alcohol and a new male partner.

Although questions could be raised about the focus of intervention prior to accommodation, and the degree to which social workers attempted to establish a partnership with the woman before using 'threats', the high levels of accommodation of children in this sample do not necessarily suggest that children were being inappropriately accommodated. Rather, male violence created a particularly vulnerable group of women and

children. In this sample it was frequently a factor associated with mothers losing their children either temporarily or permanently. Sometimes this was a direct relationship, more often an indirect association.

In five of the situations, the man's violence towards the mother and sometimes the children was the primary reason for *actual accommodation* of children or failure to rehabilitate children to their mothers. In 1996, the last year of data collection, there was much more frequent mention in conference notes of the emotional abuse children experience through witnessing domestic violence. This suggests a marked change in practice from previous research (Maynard, 1985; Farmer and Owen, 1995), although it was in situations of more extreme physical abuse of the mother that this issue is given attention.

In 11 other situations the man's violence is not stated as the primary reason, although the impairment of the mother's abilities to parent are clearly exacerbated by the abuse she experiences from her partner. Frequently in these latter situations there is little connection made between the domestic violence and the mother's ability to care for the children. Occasionally this is legitimate. In one situation, the woman's learning disabilities and inexperience in providing care for herself were such that the child would probably have been accommodated regardless of her relationship with her partner.

Four of the families in which accommodation occurred involved children of Asian heritage. None of these children had culturally sensitive placements, nor were there link families in place to meet the identity needs of these children. Such problems with placement finding significantly worsen the impact of accommodation upon these children (Humphreys et al, 1999).

A study by NCH Action for Children (Abrahams, 1994) indicated that 74% of women in the sample were concerned that if they spoke honestly to professionals about domestic violence their children might be taken away. This fear proved a significant barrier to help-seeking on their part. The figures in this study confirm, rather than alleviate, women's worst fears about social services intervention when they themselves are also experiencing violence and abuse. While it could be argued that other local authorities may have a different pattern of intervention, where the accommodation of children or threats of accommodation occurred in fewer cases, the strongly-held fear that women may risk losing their children is one that has a pervasive hold on the public psyche. It is a belief exploited by perpetrators who frequently use this as a key threat in silencing and stalling women's help-seeking. 'I'll tell them what a rotten mother you are' is a key theme in an abuser's repertoire of threats, and an effective method of maintaining control.

Previous research in the area of domestic violence also suggests that women in these circumstances are a high-risk group in terms of having their children accommodated (Stark and Flitcraft, 1988; Farmer and Owen, 1995). Farmer and Owen make the following comment:

> It should be noted that most of the children with the worst outcomes were living in families where there was continuing violence by the man towards his female partner. This violence was sometimes concealed from the authorities or was considered by professionals to be peripheral to their concerns. (Farmer and Owen, 1995, p 319)

This study would confirm those earlier findings, although the figures need to be understood in the context of the numbers of children accommodated as a proportion of overall child protection referrals (Gibbons et al, 1995). The research summary, *Messages from research* (DoH, 1995) indicates that of the 160,000 children referred to the child protection process, one quarter led to a meeting of professionals at a child protection conference and only 4% of children are accommodated. These figures 'hide' the numbers of children who are accommodated voluntarily, as well as the number of cases in which 'threats' are made to accommodate children. Nevertheless, the accommodation of children represents only a very small percentage of children for whom referrals are made and clearly represents the extreme end of the child protection spectrum.

Social work responses

The attitude of social workers to this association between domestic violence and child abuse varied.

One group of social workers expressed considerable distress about intervention that they knew women who were already being abused would experience as punitive, and in which effective support towards the woman had not been achieved. As one social worker said:

> "At times like these you feel your hands are tied. You know that it's punitive towards the mother, but in a case like this we are really dependent on her leaving to protect the children."

Other social workers believed the needs of the children justified a 'firm' response towards the mother at the child protection conference.

> "Our role is in relation to the children, and some of these women are just unable to put their children's interests first."

> "You have to consider the children and they can't wait forever."

Future directions

> There is a danger that, as the awareness of the impact on children of living with domestic violence rises, social work concerns could lead to well-meaning and apparently child-focused but actually intrusive and unhelpful interventions. (Mullender, 1996, p 96)

Clearly, the evidence in this research suggests a pressure for women to leave violent men and that staying in situations of domestic violence now represents a new parameter in the mother's 'failure to protect' – a shift in position from even 10 years ago when research studies documented the pressure on women by child protection workers to 'stay with the man for the sake of the children' (Maynard, 1985; Stark and Flitcraft, 1988).

The concerning pattern of high levels of accommodation of children in this sample begs a number of questions: to what extent was the man's violence the focus of intervention? Were women given resources, support and protection to help them separate should they wish this for themselves and their children? Were women required to separate and maintain separation from their partners with heavy monitoring from agencies, but minimal support? Would an earlier intervention focusing on family support, particularly addressing the issues for the child's mother, have made a difference to the outcome in many of these cases?

The following sections of this chapter discuss the form of intervention evidenced through child protection conferences with a view to exploring the questions of offender focus and support for women and children throughout this process.

Partnership, punishment or marginalisation: women and children's issues

Case example: Family 32

A child protection conference was called following an incident in which S, a 15-year-old girl, was punched in the mouth and her head banged against the wall by her stepfather. Her mother had also been the subject of assault from her husband. Prior to the child protection conference there had been conversations with S and her mother. The stepfather had declined to participate. S decided that she wanted to be present at the child protection conference and to give her views. She was well supported by both her mother and social workers in preparation for, and during, this process.

Unlike some other social services departments in Britain (see Shemmings, 1996, 1998), the practice of children presenting their views either directly or indirectly to child protection conferences was not well developed at the time of the research. Family 32 was one of only three situations in which this occurred in this sample. These examples all involved older children.

A further issue for children stemming from the child protection conference is whether the case plan took into account the assessment of the effects of violence and recommended that children be given support and counselling where appropriate.

The first chapter of this report provided a brief overview of the short- and long-term effects on children of domestic violence. The recent research study undertaken in Coventry (Hendessai, 1997) is consistent with other studies (Hughes, 1988; Abrahams, 1994; Brandon and Lewis, 1996) in reporting the effects of domestic violence on children. Careful consideration needs to be given to individual children and the ways in which they experience and respond to their home and community life.

It was therefore of concern to note that in this study, in *only two case plans were children recommended for counselling* to assist them with any issues that may have arisen for them in the context of domestic violence. This figure may be an underestimate given that there were three families in which Asian children attended groups or participated in direct work associated with identity issues. In these cases some of their family issues may have been attended to. Other children may also have had a chance to speak of their experiences under the broad rubric of 'family assessment', although if they did it is rarely mentioned in the resultant social work report. Other younger children may be attending nurseries or refuges where their specific needs may be addressed by children's workers. Generally, the particular issues for children in situations of domestic violence are not given attention, a finding consistent with the study undertaken by Brandon and Lewis (1996) which demonstrated that the effects on children witnessing domestic violence were often profound, but overlooked by social workers and the interagency case planning process. This is particularly serious both for the children who may be carrying the trauma of witnessing or directly experiencing violence, but also for their mothers, many of whom are being threatened with having their children accommodated without assessments being undertaken about the effects that they are actually experiencing and the strategies which children are using to survive in their families.

Future directions

Since this research was undertaken, there has been a proliferation of work which has developed with children, through Women's Aid and also through the children's charities, (NSPCC, NCH Action for Children, The Children's Society, Barnardo's) and

Refuge. In many areas, social services departments are commissioning work in the voluntary sector to attend to both the needs of children witnessing domestic violence as well as their mothers. Penzance, for example, has developed a partnership between the NSPCC and Women's Aid to run parallel groups for women and children in situations of domestic violence. Other projects, like NSPCC in Northampton, use the auspice of one organisation to run groups for women and children to discuss the effects of domestic violence in their lives. The Children's Society has pioneered work researching with children who have experienced domestic violence, while Dunfermline Women's Aid has been at the forefront of developing materials for children's groups (see Scottish Women's Aid) and running parallel women's groups both in its refuge and outreach centre.

Work has also developed in consulting with children prior to child protection conferences to ascertain their wishes, needs and feelings (Shemmings, 1998). Where domestic violence is an issue, considerable attention needs to be given to the safety issues for children so that they are not being placed at risk through their input. On the other hand, particularly where the offender is not in attendance and the process is minuted in ways which will not place them at risk in the future, then strategies for bringing children's views before the conference need to be actively considered. Further developments have occurred through family group conferences. However, again there are problems if such a process is being considered where domestic violence is an issue.

Domestic violence and child contact

A further issue which concerned children and strongly impacted upon their mothers in situations of domestic violence involved child contact. The arrangements for contact were not always specified at the child protection conference and there were many informal arrangements in place. In this sample, *there were five conferences in which detailed consideration was given to making contact arrangements for men who had been violent to their partners.* At times, this appeared to be a mechanism available to the conference to assert some authority over the man by specifying supervised contact arrangements in nurseries and family centres. Men (and women) on

a number of occasions used conferences to argue for greater access or unsupervised access. These were sometimes refused.

In one situation (Family 37), a man was charged with abusing his child so seriously that permanent brain damage had resulted. The child now lives with learning disabilities as a result of abuse. This man was already a Schedule 1 offender who had seriously abused a similarly aged child in a prior relationship. He had also been reported to the police for domestic violence offences. Regardless of these issues, supervised contact was arranged for him with his other child even prior to the court ruling (which in this case did not result in a conviction).

There is little detail given of the evaluation of contact arrangements so it is difficult to ascertain the extent to which post-separation violence continued as a result of contact arrangements. This is, however, an issue which is now being raised by research evidence which shows that child contact arrangements are a primary site for post-separation violence (Hester and Radford, 1996; Humphreys, 1999). Hester and Radford (1996) in their research on child contact conclude that although the majority of the women interviewed in their study wanted their children to have contact with their father after separation, the contact arrangements tended not to work. Only seven out of 53 cases in England and two out of 24 cases in Denmark were eventually set up so that there was no further abuse and harassment of the mother or the children. The contact ultimately did not work because of the men's continuing violence and abuse. The majority of women were assaulted by their husbands/partners after leaving the relationship and all of the post-separation violence was linked in some way to child contact.

These are significant findings which child protection workers who are wanting to encourage separation between women, children and their violent partners need to take into greater account. In this process they are clearly unassisted by the Children Act 1989 in which there is a presumption in favour of contact for the child with both parents, with little consideration given of the consequences and harm which might result from such contact (Parker and Eaton, 1994).

An advisory sub-committee to the Lord Chancellor's Department has now issued a consultation paper on *Contact between children and violent parents: The question of parental contact in cases where there is domestic violence* (1999). This provides a comprehensive outline of the law and complex issues raised by child contact in the context of previous or current domestic violence. Public consultation on the issue has been invited and an interdepartmental working party is now meeting to explore a range of options which might allow the issues of domestic violence and child abuse associated with child contact to be taken into account. Currently, there are considerable difficulties for child protection workers where protective action is not supported by legislation.

Practical and emotional support for women

The level of emotional and practical support available to women and children when faced with difficult decisions about their future is constantly referred to as a crucial factor in determining the confidence with which women pursue their options (Mullender, 1996; Abrahams, 1994). Comments from women on the support that they valued from social workers included: being listened to and understood; a preparedness to address the issues which they identified as important in their lives and those of their children; sympathy and compassion; and practical help (Farmer and Owen, 1995, p 227). Black women frequently require additional information and support on their legal and immigration rights (Mama, 1989; Bhatti-Sinclair, 1994) as well as sensitive counselling on weighing up the dilemmas for the woman and her children should she decide to leave her husband and risk not only his ire but, for some women, the rejection of their community (Imam, 1994).

In this sample, there was considerable pressure placed on women to separate or remain separated from violent men if they wanted to retain residency with their children. However, the practical and emotional supports which might have made this possible were often inadequate. For example, one woman, after a particularly vicious attack on herself and her children, was initially very keen to move and not have her partner back. However, in spite of intensive support given by the social worker, the attempt to find her refuge accommodation out of Coventry in adjoining local authorities (where she could continue to have family support), from where she could be rehoused, proved fruitless. Another woman, again with good social work support, was by contrast successfully rehoused and has moved out of a very violent relationship. Some of the difference in outcomes for these two women were related to different policies concerning emergency prioritisation by the respective housing associations.

It also appeared to be evidence of good practice that in *four situations where the mother was not a threat to the child, decisions were deliberately made by conference not to register the child* but to bring in a support package for the woman and children involved. A further situation involved the immediate deregistration but continued support for a woman when she separated and moved to a refuge (Family 40). These support packages included the allocation of a keyworker or student social worker. The successful work with the woman rehoused in the above example was such a case.

This, however, begs the question of whether the child should have been the focus of an investigation and child protection conference in the first instance. *Every worker who was interviewed felt that the work on their case should have been streamed into a Section 47 enquiry.* This highlights the point made very clearly by Parton (1996), that any re-balancing of child protection work and family support requires an understanding of how decisions are initially made by social workers to undertake a Section 47 enquiry and assess the child protection risks to children. The legacy of 20 years of child death inquiries which have constantly supported a trend to greater proceduralism and greater legalism is difficult to turn around to a system which prioritises support for children in need. Such a shift relies on a change in management priorities and parallel support and resourcing for team leaders and social workers to divert families from Section 47 enquiries.

Partnership with women

The extent to which women are consulted and in agreement with the plans made at conference is very unclear from case conference minutes. On four out of 32 occasions it was recorded that one or both parents were *not* in agreement with the plans. This often involved decisions about limited contact with children already accommodated, or where children were not being returned to their families.

Following one strategy meeting it was recorded that the mother was strongly in accord with the meeting's recommendations (Family 30). This case had one of the most successful outcomes in the sample where the woman worked closely with a very supportive social worker to separate from her partner and to be rehoused with her children.

There seemed little indication in other conferences of the women's attitude to the recommendations, even when it involved excluding the man from the family home. In this situation the recommendations of conference are very dependent upon the woman's cooperation. Potentially, it is a situation where her ideas about the prevention of further violence and alcohol abuse are often in tandem with those of the professionals. Women consistently say that they want the abuse to cease (McGibbon and Kelly, 1989), and having a group of professionals who she could perceive as having more power than her in relation to the man *could* give the woman greater support, resources and leverage than she has when trying to act alone. However, this decision-making process, particularly when it is not based in extensive conversations between the social worker and the mother prior to conference, can be experienced by women as punitive and lead to alienation rather than a sense of support.

Future directions

Good practice in this area will be dependent upon the extent to which statutory organisations are prepared to recognise that effective child protection also entails strategies to support and protect the child's mother from abuse. Simply heightening the awareness that children are abused directly or indirectly when living with domestic violence may only lead to punitive practices towards their mothers unless active consideration is given to more woman-centred practices which recognise her need for support.

Safety planning and advocacy in partnership with women and their children provides the basis for work with women in this area. This work involves

detailed consideration of the strengths and safety strategies that women and their children may already be using; an assessment of the abuser-engendered dangers; an exploration of women's fears and concerns in relation to her children herself, and the abuser; and the risks and meaning which she associates with either leaving or staying. Safety planning recognises that a woman's assessment of risks will encompass a range of considerations in relation to her race, ethnicity, immigration status, the cultural meanings for her and her children of separation from a marriage and single parenthood, as well as other social issues such as age, access to material resources, health and disability and other social influences (Davies et al, 1998). It is a process which may differ quite markedly from risk assessment, which often implies professionals' assessment of a situation. Safety planning at its heart involves a partnership and exploration with the woman without an initial presumption about where the best interests for the woman and her children lie. At times this process may not be possible as the danger to the children may be immediate, or it may only be possible with an independent advocate or worker from a voluntary agency.

Consultation prior to child protection conferences for both women and children is essential when domestic violence is an issue. Wherever possible, information about domestic violence should be bought to the conference by the police, so that the already publicly recorded incidents are documented. In this way, the woman's private conversations with workers about the violence she is experiencing are not available to the abuser and therefore do not place her in further danger following the conference.

Sensitivity to the particular needs and appropriate support for Asian women will also need attention. A community development approach which takes into account the specific local circumstances and develops appropriate and accessible services will be a high priority (Pryke and Thomas, 1998). However, assessment which is sensitive to the interpreting needs of the situation, which takes a more holistic approach to the woman's needs (Humphreys et al, 1999), and which takes into account the vulnerability to abuse from more than one person in the family will provide specific challenges to statutory workers and others in the interagency network.

Assessments and packages of support will need to give consideration to the needs of women as well as children. In this sample, there tended to be an over-emphasis on monitoring and assessment, and less attention to the actual provision of support services for women and children which would assist them with the process of securing their safety, in the aftermath of domestic violence. Future directions will need to redress this imbalance.

A shift towards family support (Section 17) and away from child protection enquiries (Section 47) will not occur without a change in resource allocation and the development of programmes to which women, children and men can be diverted. Moreover, until front-line workers feel sufficiently supported by senior management, they will be unable to trust that a decision to provide family support rather than an investigation and multiagency conference will constitute an adequate intervention. Areas such as Oxfordshire and Northampton are developing guidelines to look at these assessment issues alongside guidance developed by the DoH. However, practice in this area has generally been slow to develop, and much of the work to re-balance the focus of statutory child welfare is still the subject of restructuring and experimentation (Parton, 1997).

Attendance by domestic violence offenders at child protection conferences

Case example: Family 5

The M family is an Asian family with three children. A child protection conference was convened following an investigation which revealed that the father's drinking and violence towards his wife was escalating and his daughter had been bitten during so-called 'rough' play. Discussions with the mother prior to conference revealed concerns about the abuse to which she was subjected. She was becoming increasingly fearful that the mental health problems she had experienced

previously would return. At the conference, the police listed the incidents at the home which they had been called to, and the range of charges which the man had incurred. In this way, it was the public police information, not information directly from the mother, which allowed domestic violence to be placed on the conference agenda for consideration.

The issue of the attendance at child protection conferences of men who are violent towards their partners is a complex one. Farmer and Owen (1995) point out that by the end of their study, twice as many cases of male violence were known about than had been indicated at the initial child protection conferences. They also draw attention to the fact that women in situations of domestic violence often felt they had no choice but to 'ally themselves publicly with their partners' for fear of recrimination. This study by Farmer and Owen suggests that domestic violence and how it is managed, or not managed, by professionals may be a significant issue in the child protection process which is currently being ignored. Bell (1996) and Savas (1996) similarly draw attention to the need to specify who the professional/parent partnership is with, and that it may be limited in situations of domestic violence. Savas (1996) showed that professionals were markedly less able to discuss child protection issues where they either directly feared the man's violence, or feared the repercussions on the woman of such a discussion.

In 11 cases in this sample, where male violence towards the mother was/or had been an issue, the father attended the case conference either alone or with the mother present. In one case the domestic violence was from a former partner and not a current issue.

In nine of these cases domestic violence was not mentioned in the case plan, and if it was discussed at conference the issue was avoided or minimised. Even in the case mentioned above (Family 5), the conference moved on to focus on the man's alcohol problems rather than his violence.

In a further two cases, the way in which the domestic violence was discussed and recommendations made in the case plan would have put the woman at risk of further abuse. For example, one of the workers gave out information that the mother confided in her after incidents of domestic violence, that her partner was reluctant for her to go to the women's group so she didn't attend, and that incidents of abuse were increasing with her attempts at greater independence.

There are a number of conflicting issues which emerge over case conference attendance. On the one hand, Department of Health guidance encourages partnership with, and participation from, parents at all points in the child protection process and the research generally demonstrates that participation by mothers and fathers is valued and effective (Thoburn et al, 1995). The issue is further couched in terms of rights and natural justice for mothers and fathers whose children are the subject of professional discussions in public forums. The specific issues which arise in inviting children to such forums when domestic violence is an issue has been given comparatively less consideration.

On the other hand, most studies which explore women's experiences of domestic violence suggest that placing women in situations in which they are asked to talk about family/personal issues with the offender present, at best silences her opinion or at worst puts her in situations of increased danger (Hester and Radford, 1996). These studies refer usually to mediation or counselling practice and were issues which were successfully fought when the new Family Law Bill was being developed. Child protection practice has the added complexity of a strong tendency to make men who are violent or abusive invisible, focusing all attention/responsibility upon the mother in the family (Milner, 1993). This tendency possibly increases if men are *not* present at conferences. It is clearly an issue which should involve careful negotiation with the woman prior to the conference about her wishes and the risks she may face if violence towards her is discussed or not discussed and the problems of having a man present who has been violent towards her.

Future directions

Practice in the area is increasingly varied. Areas in which there has been a sustained interagency strategy focused on domestic violence have shifted to providing separate times at the conference for men and women, or only inviting the woman,

particularly following separation. In some situations this will not be an option without further endangering the woman. Particular cultural practices in some religious or ethnic groups will not allow the woman to attend a public forum, such as a child protection conference, without her husband present (Atkar et al, 1997). In these circumstances, careful consultation with the woman prior to the conference about her safety and how information should be shared needs to be discussed. Conference chairs will need to consider the usefulness of a conference in which full information sharing by either workers or the woman involved is not possible. In one situation in this sample (Family 30), in which a particularly violent man was involved, a strategy meeting with the woman present was convened. This provided a particularly good partnership with the woman, and each professional participant at the strategy meeting left with a specific commitment to an intervention which would support either the woman or child involved.

Central to any strategy involving domestic violence and child abuse is the need to systematically monitor for domestic violence. Farmer and Owen (1995) and Hester and Pearson (1998) both show in their research that there was a dramatic increase in the number of families in which workers knew domestic violence occurred once questions about violence began to be asked. During any child abuse enquiry, or assessment for family support, the issue of domestic violence will need to be sensitively explored. In this sample, it was clear that in some cases, the police bought knowledge of domestic violence to the conference, as the social worker had not mentioned it either in the report to conference or in case notes. The issue had not been on the social worker's agenda for exploration. Yet the issue of violence towards the child's mother is clearly one which is significant in any enquiry about child abuse and affects the way in which information can be safely shared.

The shift towards both 'assessment conferences' for family support and family group conferences raises particular issues in relation to domestic violence. While initially it was agreed that family group conferences were unsuitable venues when violence towards the mother was an issue, there has been a recent shift away from this consensus. There are dangers associated with this shift. Offenders have often groomed the family environment to support their definition of the situation. Much of the research on Asian women and domestic violence shows that women are being abused not just by their husbands, but by other members of her husband's family (Hendessai, 1999). Within these family structures, women may find themselves doubly abused and disempowered, rather than strengthened through the process. To an extent, this may be dependent upon a number of factors: the work undertaken with the extended family prior to conference; whether it is only the risks to the child which are centralised, or whether the mother's experience of abuse is recognised as both a concern for her as well as her children; and how the issues of safety and support for the mother as well as the children are ensured.

The evidence from this research showed that it was all too easy for professionals to collude with the man's violence through avoidance, minimisation or slipping the focus onto the woman. The nub of the problem lies in how a process can be established which places responsibility on the offender for his violence, while at the same time not increasing the danger to women and children.

Raising the stakes: violence against workers

8

An issue which is frequently overlooked in discussions of child protection is worker protection. A survey of workers employed by social services in Britain showed that this was a relatively dangerous occupational choice (Pahl, 1999). Residential workers were those most at risk of physical and verbal abuse although field social workers were also experiencing significant levels of violence (approximately one quarter had been physically attacked, almost half had been threatened with violence and approximately 80% had been shouted at or insulted in their current job). *Community Care* began a campaign for safety in social work (*No Fear*, August 1999) in response to the endemic problems in the social welfare field which are increasingly coming to light (Balloch et al, 1999).

It has been suggested that unless workers are much better protected and supervised, it is unlikely that practices which collude with, or minimise, male violence will change. Research by Stanley and Goddard (1997) shows that the consistency with which minimisation of violence occurs in the files of social workers suggests that the dynamics of survival when under severe threat, which often affect women who experience violence from known men, may also be affecting workers. They give as an example a sample of 50 workers who recalled on average only half of the extent of violence recorded in their current cases. Working in situations in which violence is a threat or a possibility is often best survived through collusion with the man, agreeing to his definitions of the situation, and minimising in the worker's mind the possible risks they face. This is clearly not the total picture. Training and awareness do bring changes which suggest that the organisational environment

and the attitude of managers to the issue of domestic violence has an impact on practice (Mullender, 1996). Nevertheless, placing workers in situations in which they are vulnerable to physical and verbal abuse and lack good supervision will inevitably lead to poor practice.

In this sample there were *11 reported instances of abusive incidents to workers.*

Not all incidents involved social workers and only half of the incidents involved the man who was abusive to his partner or ex-partner. Most of the incidents involved verbal abuse or threats, and in one instance racial abuse towards a black social worker.

On two occasions, workers (one community psychiatric nurse and residential workers at an assessment centre) reported incidents in which the woman was assaulted in front of them and in which they felt powerless to intervene without increasing the violence towards the woman. There was one incident in which a woman physically assaulted a worker.

In this sample, particular risks appeared to be involved when children were being accommodated or decisions had been made not to rehabilitate the children to the family. Generally, there was a tendency to underestimate the risks posed by women and other family members to workers. In both teams in the study, particularly when children were to be accommodated, these risks were prevalent.

Many workers commented that the public face the

man presented to them was often at odds with what was happening in the home environment. Workers made statements such as "butter wouldn't melt in his mouth", "he was always so smooth", "he never threatened us", "just once in the assessment he got up walked around and made a veiled threat, that was the only clue he gave of what he might be like to his wife". There was an awareness by workers that they were being 'hoodwinked' by manipulative men whose record of violence against their wives belied their smooth talk to workers. However, the evidence of minimisation in the sample, and the number of times that abusive men were seen as essential to family functioning suggests that these manipulations were also often quite effective.

Future directions

In this study workers (and child protection conferences) avoided abuse from men by avoiding men, or avoiding challenging men. Women were much more the focus of social work attention, an issue that has frequently been evidenced in other studies (Maynard, 1985; Farmer and Owen, 1995). Should there be a shift to more proactive work with men, there would need to be an attendant shift in the security offered workers.

Employers would need to take more seriously their responsibilities under the 1974 Health and Safety at Work Act, in which under Section 2 (1) they have a duty 'to ensure so far as is reasonably practicable, the health, safety and welfare at work of employees'. While most social services organisations already have written health and safety guidance, the extent to which a 'culture of safety' is established within an organisation is very variable.

Training of all workers in an organisation is key to good practice. Reception staff need to be as aware of safety guidelines as field staff and managers. The physical layout of a building, the accessibility of alarms and not leaving a staff member alone to open or lock up the building at night are important preventative measures. Other simple strategies include personal alarms, mobile phones, staff notifying departure and return times when making home visits, and seniors waiting until everyone is back from visits before leaving the office (Mullender, 1996, p 77).

Police may need to be much more involved in case plans, not just the investigation. Social workers should not visit homes by themselves where violence is an ongoing issue or where the situation is unknown. Staffing levels therefore need to be such that 'doubling up' on home visits is not considered a luxury only kept for the most extreme cases, and office visits need to be arranged more frequently and wherever possible.

It should be assumed that the fear of violence will have a considerable influence on individual work where domestic violence is an issue. Supervision sessions should always involve probing questions on the effects of violence on the workers' intervention and the development of strategies to counter these effects.

Local authorities such as Cheshire have developed practice in this area (*Guidance to staff on violence by clients – Policy, practice and procedures*). These guidelines take into account both individual and organisational issues and establish a framework in which abuse towards workers is openly discussed and countered.

Conclusion

9

This research explored the patterns of decision making and the context in which those decisions were made for 93 children whose lives were affected by domestic violence and who were the subject of child protection conferences between 1994-96. It highlighted issues that concerned the relationship between child protection workers, women who were the subject of domestic violence and men who were violent towards women and sometimes their children.

The research suggests that practice in this area is both changing and very varied, with examples of good practice as well as some worrying examples of poor practice. However, the work of individual workers and interventions within child protection conferences needs to be understood in the context of teams and a department which were in a constant state of being restructured over the period of the research. Moreover, there is a wider context in which this work is happening. This is namely discussions about re-balancing the relationship between family support and child protection, heightened concerns about the accommodation of children (Utting, 1997), restructuring of the relationship between health and social services, and stringent cost-cutting to social services in many areas. In this atmosphere of change, tackling heightened areas of concern and responding to these within the parameters of the wider shifts in practice and structures is understandably complex. Increasingly, domestic violence is being named as a risk factor in the lives of children. The ability of social services departments to respond with appropriate protection for children and support for women, and to place responsibility upon men has

been limited by a number of factors. Some of these include:

- A dilemma of 'family support' without either clarity or resources which would underpin the notion that in this area, good child protection requires concerted attention to the protection of the woman. This is not to suggest that children's wishes should be conflated with their mother's. The most difficult situations occur where the child has both a mother and a father who are unsuitable to look after them. However, frequently decisions, particularly about 'bad mothers', are taken without enough support for a context in which 'good enough mothering' may be possible. (The good practice illustrated in some of these case examples exemplifies what can be possible when work in this area is prioritised.)

- A lack of awareness by workers of the effects of domestic violence on the lives of women and children. Thus, the physical and mental health needs of women are frequently ignored, both in their own right and in relation to the impact this may have on their ability to look after their children. Asian women in this sample appeared to be particularly vulnerable, yet their needs in this area were frequently overlooked.

- A tendency to focus intervention/responsibility on the mother, while either avoiding or working ineffectively with fathers. These issues are compounded for Asian women whose problems of isolation, immigration status and pressures from their own communities placed them in invidious positions when threatened with the removal of their children by social services.

- Little focus on the needs of children in the aftermath of domestic violence, including the problems of contact arrangements should separation occur between the child's mother and father.

- The need for a domestic violence strategy which develops services to support women and children, so that there is less resort to the accommodation of children or the threat of accommodating children through child protection procedures.

- The continued need to develop a proactive approach to domestic violence offenders. This will include the development of effective offender programmes alongside proactive work by the police in pressing both the criminal nature of the offence and the protection needs of women and children in the face of this violence.

- The lack of attention to the safety of workers.

- The lack of awareness of the complex issues which arise for child protection conferences when men who abuse their partners are present, including the issues which arise for case planning.

In spite of the many difficulties of practice in the area of domestic violence and child abuse, many of the social workers who were interviewed were aware that they would like to improve their work in this area, and were striving to develop their practice. However, there is a need for individual practice to be supported by a management context in which the complexity of work in this area is understood and policy, resources and training developed accordingly.

Since the research was undertaken, legislation, policy and practice in the area has been given greater attention. However, a recent study *Mapping of good practice where there is domestic violence* (Joseph Rowntree Foundation, forthcoming) shows that while there has been a significant amount of innovative practice initiatives developed by the Women's Aid Federation, the children's charities and domestic violence forums, significant problems remain in the statutory childcare sector. Few local authorities were 'mainstreaming' the issue into their fieldwork teams and tackling the barriers which have traditionally occurred to the development of good practice in this area. Fortunately, as this

project has illustrated, good practice can occur through dedicated workers with a grasp of the issues surrounding domestic violence and child abuse. The challenge for social services departments is to build on both individual and national impetus in this area to improve intervention and the services to children, women and men where domestic violence is an issue.

References

Abrahams, C. (1994) *Hidden victims*, London: NCH Action for Children.

Atkar, S., Ghataora, R. with Baldwin, N. and Thanki, V. (1997) *Hifazat Surukhia: Keeping safe, child protection and family support needs of Asian children and families*, Final Report, NSPCC, Wales and Midlands Region and University of Warwick.

Ball, M. (1995) *Domestic violence and social care: A report on two conference held by the Social Services Inspectorate*, London: SSI, DoH.

Balloch, S., McLean, J. and Fisher, M. (eds) (1999) *Social services: Working under pressure*, Bristol: The Policy Press.

Barron, J. (1990) *Not worth the paper...?*, Bristol: Women's Aid Federation of England.

Bell, M. (1996) 'An account of the experiences of 51 families involved in an initial child protection conference', *Child and Family Social Work*, vol 1, pp 43-6.

Bhatti-Sinclair, K. (1994) 'Asian women and violence from male partners', in C. Lupton and T. Gillespie (eds) *Working with violence*, Basingstoke: Macmillan.

BMA (British Medical Association) (1998) *Domestic violence: A health care issue?*, London: BMA.

Bowker, L., Arbitell, M. and McFerron, R. (1988) 'On the relationship between wife beating and child abuse', in K. Yllo and M. Bograd (eds) *Feminist perspectives on wife abuse*, London: Sage Publications, pp 158-75.

Brandon, M. and Lewis, A. (1996) 'Significant harm and children's experiences of domestic violence', *Child and Family Social Work*, vol 1, pp 33-42.

Burke, C. (1999) 'Redressing the balance in child protection intervention in the context of domestic violence', in J. Breckenridge and L. Laing (eds) *Challenging silence: Innovative responses to sexual and domestic violence*, Sydney: Allen and Unwin, pp 256-68.

Burton, S., Regan, L. and Kelly, L. (1998) *Supporting women and challenging men: Lessons from the Domestic Violence Intervention Project*, Bristol: The Policy Press.

Campbell, J. (1995) 'Prediction of homicide of, and by battered women', in J. Campbell (ed) *Assessing dangerousness: Violence by sexual offenders, batterers and child abusers*, Thousand Oaks: Sage Publications, p 5-15.

Choudry, S. (1996) *Pakistani women's experiences of domestic violence in Great Britain*, Research Finding No 43, London: Home Office Research and Statistics Directorate.

Coffey, A. and Atkinson, P. (1996) *Making sense of qualitative data*, London: Sage Publications.

Conner, K. and Ackerley, G. (1994) 'Alcohol-related battering: developing treatment strategies', *Journal of Family Violence*, vol 9, no 2, pp 143-55.

Davies, J. with Lyon, E. and Monti-Catania, D. (1998) *Safety planning with battered women: Complex lives/difficult choices*, London: Sage Publications.

Diggins, M. and Mazey, K. (1998) *Crossing bridges: The impact of parental mental ill health on child welfare – A training pack*, London: DoH.

Dobash, R.E. and Dobash, R. (1980) *Violence against wives*, Buckingham: Open Books.

DoH (Department of Health) (1995) *Messages from research*, London: HMSO.

DoH (1998a) *Quality protects: Transforming children's services*, London: Crown Copyright.

DoH (1998b) *Working together to safeguard children*, A Consultation Paper, London: The Stationery Office.

DoH (1999a) *Framework for the assessment of children in need and their families: Consultation draft*, London: Crown Copyright.

DoH (1999b) *Mapping quality in children's services: An evaluation of the local responses to the Quality Protects programme: National overview report*, London: Crown Copyright.

Eberle, P. (1982) 'Alcohol abusers and non-users: a discriminant analysis of differences between two subgroups of batterers', *Journal of Health and Social Behaviour*, vol 23, pp 260-71.

Eekelaar, J. and Katz, S. (1978) *Family violence: An international interdisciplinary study*, London: Butterworths.

Fagan, R., Barnett, D. and Patton, J. (1998) 'Reasons for alcohol abuse in maritally violent men', *American Journal*, vol 14, pp 371-92.

Farmer, E. (1997) 'Protection and child welfare: striking the balance', in N. Parton (ed) *Child protection and family support*, London: Routledge, pp 146-64.

Farmer, E. and Owen, M. (1995) *Child protection practice: Private risks and public remedies*, London: HMSO.

Forman, J. (1995) *Is there a correlation between child sexual abuse and domestic violence? An exploratory study of the links between child sexual abuse and domestic violence in a sample of intrafamilial child sexual abuse cases*, Glasgow: Women's Support Project.

Gelles, R. (1993) 'Alcohol and other drugs are associated with violence – They are not its cause', in R. Gelles and D. Loseke (eds) *Current controversies on family violence*, London: Sage Publications, pp 182-96.

Gelles, R. and Harrop, J. (1989) 'Violence and psychological distress among women', *Journal of Interpersonal Violence*, vol 4, pp 400-20.

Gibbons, J., Conroy, S. and Bell, C. (1995) *Operating the child protection system: A study of child protection practice in English local authorities*, London: HMSO.

Grace, S. (1995) *Policing domestic violence in the 1990s*, London: HMSO.

Grounds, A. (1995) 'Risk assessment and management in clinical context', in J. Crichton (ed) *Psychiatric patient violence: Risk and response*, London: Duckworth.

Hague, G., Hester, M., Humphreys, C., Mullender, A., Abrahams, H. and Lowe, P. (2000: forthcoming) *Mapping good practice in working with families where there is domestic violence*, Bristol: The Policy Press.

Hanmer, J., Griffiths, S. and Jerwood, D. (1999) *Arresting evidence: Domestic violence and repeat victimisation*, London: Crown Publishing.

Hendessai, M. (1997) *Voices of children witnessing domestic violence: A form of child abuse*, Report of a research project on the issues and needs of children who live with domestic violence in Coventry, Coventry: Coventry Domestic Violence Focus Group.

Hendessai, M. (1999) *A space for us*, Milton Keynes, PO Box 790, Milton Keynes MK2 3YZ.

Hester, M. and Pearson, C. (1998) *From periphery to centre: Domestic violence in work with abused children*, Bristol: The Policy Press.

Hester, M. and Radford, J. (1996) *Domestic violence and child contact arrangements in England and Denmark*, Bristol: The Policy Press.

Hester, M., Pearson, C. and Harwin, N. (1999) *Making an impact: A reader*, London: Jessica Kingsley .

Horwath, J. and Shardlow, S. (forthcoming) *Making links: Assessment and role across social work specialisms*, Lyme Regis: Russell House Publishing.

Hughes, H. (1988) 'Psychological and behavioural correlates of family violence in child witnesses and victims', *American Journal of Orthopsychiatry*, vol 58, no 1, pp 75-9.

Hughes, R. (1996) 'The Department of Health research studies in child protection: a response to Parton', *Child and Family Social Work*, vol 1, no 2, pp 115-18.

Humphreys, C. (1999) 'The judicial alienation syndrome: failures to respond to post-separation violence', *Family Law Journal*, vol 29, pp 313-16.

Humphreys, C. and Kaye, M. (1997) 'Third Party Protection Orders: opportunities, ambiguities and traps', *Journal of Social Welfare and Family Law*, vol 19, no 4, pp 403-21.

Humphreys, C., Atkar, S. and Baldwin, N. (1999) 'Discrimination in child protection work: recurring themes in work with Asian families', *Child and Family Social Work*, vol 4, no 4, pp 283-92.

Hunter, J. (1999) 'Possible child abuse cases being ignored', *Community Care*, 18-24 March, p 3.

Imam, U. (1994) 'Asian children and domestic violence', in A. Mullender and R. Morley (eds) *Children living with domestic violence*, London: Whiting & Birch.

Ingram, R. (1993) *Violence from known men: Women and mental health*, Leeds: Leeds Inter-Agency Project (Women and Violence).

Jacobson, A. and Richardson, B. (1987) 'Assault experiences of 100 psychiatric inpatients: evidence of need for routine inquiry', *American Journal of Psychiatry*, vol 144, pp 908-13.

James, G. (1994) *Discussion report for ACPC conference 1994: Study of Working Together 'Part 8' Reports*, ACPC Series, Report No 1, London: DoH.

Jenkins, A. (1989) *Invitations to responsibility*, Adelaide, Australia: Dulwich Centre Publications.

Kelly, L. (1998) 'The extent of domestic violence: consequences for children', in *Violence between parents: Children as victims*, Report from the Michael Sieff Foundation, HW Fisher and Company.

Kelly, L. (1999) *Domestic violence matters: An evaluation of a development project*, Home Office Study 188, London: The Stationery Office.

Kurz, D. and Stark, E. (1988) 'Not so benign neglect: the medical response to battering', in K. Yllo and M. Bograd (eds) *Feminist perspectives on wife abuse*, London: Sage Publications, pp 249-68.

Lang, A., Goeckner, D., Adesso, B. and Marlatt, G. (1975) 'Effects of alcohol on aggression in male social drinkers', *Journal of Abnormal Psychology*, vol 84, pp 508-18.

Lloyd, S. (1995) 'Social work and domestic violence', in P. Kingston and B. Penhale (1995) *Family violence and the caring professions*, Basingstoke: Macmillan.

Lord Chancellor's Department (1999) *Consultation paper on contact between children and violent parents: The question of parental contact in cases where there is domestic violence*, London: Lord Chancellor's Department.

MacAndrew, C. and Edgerton, R. (1969) *Drunken comportment: A social explanation*, Chicago, IL: Aldine.

McGibbon, A. and Kelly, L. (1989) *Abuse in the home: Advice and information*, London: London Borough of Hammersmith and Fulham.

Mama, A. (1989) *The hidden struggle: Statutory and voluntary sector responses to violence against black women in the home*, London: London Race and Housing Research Unit.

Mayhew, P., Aye Maung, N. and Mirrlees-Black, C. (1993) *The 1992 British Crime Survey*, London: HMSO.

Maynard, M. (1985) 'The response of social workers to domestic violence', in J. Pahl (ed) *Private violence and public policy*, London: Routledge, pp 125-40.

Mezey, G. (1997) 'Domestic violence and pregnancy', *British Journal of Obstetrics and Gynaecology*, vol 104, pp 523-28.

Miller, J. and Glassner, B. (1997) 'The "inside" and the "outside": finding realities in interviews', in D. Silverman (ed) *Qualitative research*, London: Sage Publications, pp 99-112.

Milner, J. (1993) 'A disappearing act: the differing career paths of fathers and mothers in child protection investigations', *Critical Social Policy*, vol 13, pp 48-61.

Mirrlees-Black, C. (1999) *Domestic violence: Findings from a new British Crime Survey self-completion questionnaire*, Home Office Research Study 191, London: Home Office.

Mirrlees-Black, C., Mayhew, P. and Percy, A. (1996) *The British Crime Survey 1996*, London: Home Office.

Mooney, J. (1994) *The hidden figure: Domestic violence in North London*, London: London Borough of Islington, Police and Crime Prevention Unit.

Mullender, A. (1996) *Rethinking domestic violence: The social work and probation response*, London: Routledge.

Mullender, A. and Morley, R. (1994) *Children living with domestic violence*, London: Whiting & Birch.

Mullender, A., Debbonaire, T., Hague, G., Kelly, L. and Malos, E. (1998) 'Working with children in women's refuges', *Child and Family Social Work*, vol 3, no 2, pp 87-98.

National Strategy on Violence Against Women (1993) Canberra: Australian Government Publishing.

Newham Asian Women's Project (1995) *Annual Report*, PO Box 225, London.

O'Hara, M. (1994) 'Child deaths in contexts of domestic violence', in A. Mullender and R. Morley (1994) *Children living with domestic violence*, London: Whiting & Birch.

Orr, J. (1984) 'Violence against women', *Nursing Times*, April 25, pp 34-6.

Pahl, J. (1995) 'Health professionals and violence against women', in P. Kingston and B. Penhale (eds) *Family violence and the caring professions*, Basingstoke: Macmillan.

Pahl, J. (1999) 'Coping with physical violence and verbal abuse', in S. Balloch., J. McLean and M. Fisher (eds) *Social services: Working under pressure*, Bristol: The Policy Press, pp 87-106.

Parker, J. and Eaton, D. (1994) 'Opposing contact', *Family Law Journal*, November, pp 636-41.

Parkinson, P. and Humphreys, C. (1998) 'Children who witness domestic violence: the implications for child protection', *Child and Family Law Quarterly*, vol 10, no 2, pp 147-59.

Parton, N. (1996) 'Child protection, family support and social work: a critical appraisal of the Department of Health studies in child protection', *Child and Family Social Work*, vol 1, no 1, pp 3-11.

Parton, N. (ed) (1997) *Child protection and family support: Tensions, contractions and possibilities*, London: Routledge.

Patel, M. (1997) *Domestic violence and deportation*, London: Southall Black Sisters.

Pense, E. (1987) *In our best interest: A process for personal and social change*, Duluth, MN: Minnesota Program Development Inc.

Pryke, J. and Thomas, T. (1998) *Domestic violence and social work*, Aldershot: Ashgate Publishing Co.

Ross, S. (1996) 'Risk of physical abuse to children of spouse abusing parents', *Child Abuse and Neglect*, vol 20, no 7, pp 589-98.

Sashidaran, S. (1989) 'Schizophrenia or just black', *Community Care*, no 783, pp 14–16.

Savas, D. (1996) 'Parental participation in case conferences', *Child and Family Law Quarterly*, vol 8, no 1, pp 57–64.

Shemmings, D. (1996) *Children's involvement in child protection conferences*, Social Work Monograph Series, Norwich: University of East Anglia.

Shemmings, D. (1998) *In on the act: Involving young people in family support and child protection*, Norwich: University of East Anglia Publications.

SNAP (Scottish Needs Assessment Programme) Women's Health Network (1997) *Domestic violence*, Glasgow: SNAP.

Sonkin, D. (1985) 'The male batterer: an overview', in D. Sonkin, D. Martin and L. Walker (eds) *The male batterer: A treatment approach*, New York, NY: Springer.

Stanko, E., Crisp, D., Hale, C. and Lucraft, H. (1998) *Counting the costs: Estimating the impact of domestic violence in the London Borough of Hackney*, Swindon: Crime Concern.

Stanley, J. and Goddard, C. (1997) 'Failures in child protection: a case study', *Child Abuse Review*, vol 6, no 1, pp 46–54.

Stanley, N. and Penhale, B. (1999) 'The mental health problems of mothers experiencing the child protection system: identifying needs and appropriate responses', *Child Abuse Review*, vol 8, no 1, pp 34–45.

Stark, E. (1984) *The battering syndrome: Social knowledge, social therapy and abuse of women*, Binghamton, NY: State University of New York-Binghamton.

Stark, E. and Flitcraft, A. (1988) 'Women and children at risk: a feminist perspective on child abuse', *International Journal of Health Services*, vol 18, pp 97–118.

Stark, E. and Flitcraft, A. (1996) *Women at risk: Domestic violence and women's health*, London: Sage Publications.

Tara-Chand, A. (1988) *Violence against women by known men*, Training Pack, Leeds Interagency Project.

Tham, S., Ford, T. and Wilkinson, D. (1995) 'A survey of domestic violence and other forms of abuse', *Journal of Mental Health*, vol 4, pp 317–21.

Thoburn, J., Lewis, A. and Shemmings, D. (1995) *Paternalism or partnership? Family involvement in the child protection process*, London: HMSO.

Utting, W. (1997) *People like us*, London: HMSO.

Victim Support (1992) *Domestic violence: Report of a National Inter-Agency Working Party on Domestic Violence*, London: Victim Support.

Wilson, M. and Daly, M. (1992) *Homicide*, New York, NY: Aldine de Gruyter.

Wolfe, D., Jaffe, P., Wilson, S. and Zak, L. (1985) 'Children of battered women: the relation of child behaviour to family violence and maternal stress', *Journal of Consulting and Clinical Psychology*, vol 53, no 5, pp 657–65.

Wolfe, D., Sak, L., Wilson, S. and Jaffe, P. (1986) 'Child witnesses to violence between parents: critical issues in behavioural and social adjustment', *Journal of Abnormal Child Psychology*, vol 14, no 1, pp 95–104.

Appendix: Methodology

The research project was developed in conjunction with the Child Protection Unit, Coventry Social Services, and arose out of concerns which were surfacing about child protection interventions where domestic violence was a feature of the child's family. While the Social Services Inspectorate has clearly placed the issue of domestic violence on the agenda the details of how these might be translated into practice have been slower to follow. This project was established to overview current practice, and to highlight the issues that need attention if work in this area is to be progressed.

Aims

The aims of the study were to:

- highlight the patterns which arise in child protection work when domestic violence is a feature;

- examine the patterns in the context of previous literature concerning social work responses to domestic violence in the context of child abuse;

- explore the case planning issues which arise when domestic violence is an issue.

Methodology

The project used a qualitative methodology which explored the complexity of case management. Documentary analysis of case files and semi-structured interviews with workers were undertaken to gain an understanding of child protection intervention where domestic violence featured in the child's life.

Case file analysis

The documentary analysis involved the examination of files from 32 families in which domestic violence featured as an issue. This involved 93 children who were the subject of case conferences. These were all cases which had been investigated under Section 47 of the 1989 Children Act and where a subsequent child protection conference or strategy meeting (one case) had been held. Stratified sampling occurred such that every file was examined for those Asian families from two children's and families' teams who participated in a child protection conference during a two-year period (January 1994–December 1995). Of these cases 12 involved domestic violence. The point needs to be clearly made that the disproportionate number of Asian families is due to a sampling technique that sought to highlight the particular issues faced by Asian families working with child protection professionals. The 20 non-Asian files were selected over a three-year period (January 1994–December 1996) from the same two teams. These files were selected via the Child Protection Unit, team leaders and social workers identifying files in which domestic violence was not necessarily the central issue, but where it was/had been an aspect of the child's experience in their family.

The study focused on the minutes of the most recent child protection conference and the case plan that arose as a result of the conference. The documentation of case file notes and plans both prior to, and following the case conference were then examined with particular attention to the issue of domestic violence. Themes and particular 'social facts' about both the professional intervention and family characteristics were recorded systematically by the researcher through using the same proforma for each file.

The documentary analysis, following Coffey and Atkinson (1996) used the files as the primary source of data. The files, and more specifically the minutes, represent very particular ways of constructing social reality, subject to particular conventions and codes that the child protection professionals have evolved. The accounts are partial – on occasions partial in the extreme when case notes, minutes or parts of the file could not be located! The interviews with social workers were used to triangulate with the data from the file – to confirm, contradict, interpret and add to the data.

Semi-structured interviews

Social workers who had worked with each of the families were interviewed using semi-structured interviews to clarify issues that arose in the context of the case and their own attitudes and supervision in relation to the family. In five cases, social workers were unavailable for interview. Extensive notes were taken during the interviews and checked with the social worker at the completion of the discussion. Themes and patterns that arose from both the case file analysis and the interviews were then identified and analysed (Miller and Glassner, 1997). Much of the analysis depended on a careful process of triangulation both within the file, between case notes and child protection conference minutes and between the worker's discussion and the file. The silences, gaps and anomalies around the theme of domestic violence were often as important as the text.

Further triangulation occurred with the Surukhia Project (Atkar et al, 1997), a research project that arose from concerns that Asian children may not be adequately served by current children and family services. The participant observation of the Asian researcher at child protection conferences on this project confirmed, clarified and added to the information on Asian family files. Conversely, this case file research was used as part of the Surukhia Project.

Limitations of the research

This sample represents cases that have gone forward to child protection conferences – the so-called 'heavy end' of child protection. Care therefore needs to be taken before making generalisations from these files about child protection intervention in cases of domestic violence. The work of Gibbons et al (1995) shows that of all child protection referrals only 25% result in a meeting of professionals. Nevertheless, the work that is undertaken with families at this end of the spectrum represents a significant amount of both the time and resources of social services departments and is also the most intrusive work undertaken with families. It is therefore practice that is worthy of particular consideration.

The sample is also taken from a particular social services department, and taken from files between 1994-96 which again needs to be taken into account when making generalisations. Practice both within the authority and also nationally has been subject to change since this time. It is particularly worth noting that these practices occurred in an authority where there had been virtually no training of the social workers at that time about the issues of domestic violence and child abuse and where there were no policies within the social services department which related to domestic violence. Regrettably, this is still not uncommon. Hence, there will be many elements within this research which remain relevant to current practice in the UK. The work highlights the vulnerabilities to poor practice as well as drawing attention to directions for good practice. The work is updated by illustrating practice where innovative work is developing in working with children, men and women living with domestic violence.